CREATING
Realistic Landscapes
FOR MODEL RAILWAYS

CREATING
Realistic Landscapes
FOR MODEL RAILWAYS

Tony Hill

All the best with your modelling

THE CROWOOD PRESS

First published in 2010 by
The Crowood Press Ltd
Ramsbury, Marlborough
Wiltshire SN8 2HR

www.crowood.com

This impression 2018

British Library Cataloguing-in-Publication Data
A catalogue record for this book is available from the
British Library.

ISBN 978 1 84797 219 4

Disclaimer
Power tools, glues and other tools and equipment used to
create model scenery are potentially dangerous and it is vitally
important that they are used in strict accordance with the
manufacturer's instructions. The author and the publisher do not
accept any responsibility in any manner whatsoever for any error
or omission, or any loss, damage, injury, adverse outcome, or
liability of any kind incurred as a result of the use of any of the
information contained in this book, or reliance upon it.

Typeset and designed by D & N Publishing, Baydon, Wiltshire.

Printed and bound in Malaysia by Times Offset (M) Sdn. Bhd.

DEDICATION

To Sue, my wife and friend who gives me support through
all my highs and lows.

CONTENTS

PREFACE

My formative years were spent drawing, painting and creating things from my imagination with anything that came to hand. I was generally outdoors as much as possible in those halcyon days, playing with my pals up on the hills behind my home town and building tree-houses in the local woods; this played a big part in what I do now. Little did I realize that Mother Nature was quietly planting her own seeds into my subconscious, and that all that playing was to give me a love of the countryside, and trees in particular.

My working life took me into carpentry and joinery, and during this period I worked and made friends with a woodman on the estate where I was working. What he showed and taught me about the life of a woodland has stood me in good stead ever since.

Modelling railways was a natural progression for me as – like so many of my contemporaries in those days – I had lain on the floor with a train set and imagined being on that little train, making an imaginary journey. In due course I had a family of my own, and at about my son's third birthday I rekindled that love and built a train set for him. My enthusiasm didn't stop and I soon joined the local model railway club. At the club I was quickly drawn to a group who were building a Welsh narrow-gauge layout. The scenery was a very attractive part for me, and I honed and refined my skills on that little railway.

Trees in those days were made mostly from lichen and wooden sticks. I did not like the look of that very much, and started to make improvements, which eventually led to demonstrating at model railway shows. At those shows people began to ask if I would like to make them a tree and how could they make a landscape on their railway? After two or three magazine articles my first book was born, added to which my own landscape model-making business has blossomed. Travelling the land and realizing customer's dreams for them is perhaps the greatest gift that could have been given to me outside my family life. When I look back I can now see where all that playing up in the woods and on the hills has led me.

The aim of this book is to enthuse you and hopefully lead you to enjoy Mother Nature whilst creating it in model form.

Happy modelling.

Tony Hill

INTRODUCTION

Over the last few years modellers have started to look for more realistic scenes in which to show off their prized models. Creating a realistic scene requires an ability to translate that which the eye sees into a model, with the added bonuses of patience and time. This book aims to enthuse and perhaps also give a wider view of our creative hobby.

Modelling is a very similar discipline to painting a picture, except that we are working in three dimensions rather than two. The following chapters deal with almost all aspects of a landscape that a modeller will come across, starting with 'the big picture' and working down to the finest detail. It is of course up to the individual modeller how far that detail is to be taken.

There are many ways of creating a good model, but at the risk of repeating the obvious it all starts with observation. I will start with a general view of the world around us, as it appears in the UK; with this as a starting point, modellers in other parts of the world will be able to observe their respective landscapes appropriately.

A really classic view, this is Monsal Head in Derbyshire, which is very often held up to be the most picturesque and evocative railway line in England. Having walked the old line a couple of times, I marvel at the engineering skills and undaunted vision of the Victorian engineers and surveyors who could see a way through this fabulous landscape.

Each chapter will start with a discussion of the materials and tools required. This will be by no means an exhaustive list, but more of a guide. Suppliers come and go, but I will list those that I am currently using at the end of this book. I have no affiliation to any, except as a happy customer.

RESEARCH

It has always been important in creating realistic landscape models to have a good knowledge of the specific area that is to be replicated. Take a good look at your chosen subject and note the colour of the topsoil: this will normally give you a good indication of the underlying geology and how the land was cut by glacial movement, then by sea, rivers, rain and wind.

Chalk, for example, is formed by the compaction of millions of crustaceans under the sea. The sea retreats and leaves an undulating landscape that is fast covered by soil/sediment brought down by streams and rivers. Vegetation then starts to grow, and shrubs and trees start to colonize the areas. The sea starts to fight back and with the help of rain and wind erodes the chalk, creating areas such as the White Cliffs of Dover. Underneath the chalk in this area there is a seam of blue clay: this acts as a skid and, when the conditions are right, there is a cliff fall that exposes fresh white chalk, capped with a dark reddish brown soil.

Fresh chalk shows quite white after a fall, but it will soon become discoloured and turn a yellowish/green shade capped by light, then dark, brown soil covering. This is the real thing.

This is the model: it shows 'fresh chalk', with the older chalk discoloured.

ABOVE: *I use a small pocket camera that just sits in the car and is popped into my pocket when walking. It will record the time and date, which is a useful aid to jogging one's memory when viewing the results.*

RIGHT: **Here are a few books that I have found to be of use in my research, but this is by no means an exhaustive representation.**

Around these areas we find a wealth of plant life appropriate to the chalky soil. With this sort of observation the start of a journey into creating realism in model form has begun. It cannot be stated often enough that to observe and understand a chosen area is paramount if we are to succeed in creating realistic models.

It has been said that one needs a certain artistic skill to create realistic model landscapes. That may be so, but I do feel that even those of modest natural talent will be able to produce plausible scenery by using the methods described in this book. A bit of forethought allied to a certain amount of groundwork in the form of 'field surveying' is necessary – this can be combined with holidays, travelling to work and so on. It is a good idea to have a small camera close to hand so that you can take pictures of things such as the colour of soil and rock in embankments and cuttings, and different types of tree, hedges, walls and the like. I also find it useful to carry a notebook to jot down anything that might be useful.

To help my modelling I use many reference books on things such as trees, dry-stone walls, hedges, shrubs, wildflowers and geology. If I don't have suitable books in my collection then I will either search online or go to the library, but I feel there is nothing like experiencing the landscape myself to get a real feel for it. One should be aware of the constraints and influences of geology, climate and farming practice. By following these rules you will avoid blunders such as creating a chalky outcrop in the English Midlands or granite cliffs at Beachy Head. I will now take a tour of Great Britain, describing loosely the relevant landscape.

SOUTHERN ENGLAND

Taking the south-east first: this is an area of chalk downs and farmland, and woods of oaks, beeches, silver birch and ash, hawthorns, crack and weeping willow. Sycamore vies with hazel and hornbeam to form the hedgerows that line country lanes, and there is the odd sessile oak. Marshlands are found in both Kent and Sussex whilst in north Kent there are chalky outcrops that have been exploited for cement. Flint is commonly used in buildings in these counties.

The start of the White Cliffs of Dover? Not quite: this is The Warren, looking east towards Dover with the railway running close to the English Channel. This stretch of cliffs lies between Folkestone and Dover in Kent; it is a very spectacular piece of coastline and demonstrates how Mother Nature can very quickly take over after a chalk slide. Looking at the centre left we can see how trees and shrubs are growing up onto the top of a chalk slip.

BELOW: The New Forest: this is an edge to an enclosure, and shows the variety of trees that thrive there. Also worthy of note are the colours that exist within a small area.

An absolutely superb model of a south Devon coastline by Robert Dudley-Cooke, where observation of the area has paid dividends in creating such a lifelike appearance. (Dave Nicholson)

Devon again: this picture shows the rolling hills of that beautiful county.

Moving towards Southampton there is chalk downland and the New Forest, where sands and clays predominate. Scots pines, alders, hemlock, silver birch and oaks are the most common trees. Wiltshire and Salisbury Plain have a thin soil coverage that necessitates farms growing cereal crops and raising sheep. Heading further west, counties such as Somerset boast a great variety in their landscape, such as where the Mendips give way to the Cheddar Gorge. As we move further west, attractive hedgerows divide up the land.

On the south-west peninsula, Dartmoor sprouts tors of granite but few trees on its vast open tracts of high ground, whilst Exmoor boasts red sandstones, which also appear on the south Devon coast. Further west, Cornwall is noted for its huge china clay waste heaps, dry-stone walls and craggy coastline dotted with beautiful sandy coves and sheltered estuaries.

THE MIDLANDS AND EAST ANGLIA

Heading north to the Midlands the landscape is really diverse. The West Midlands has a lovely rich red soil indicative of the red sandstone that runs right down to the South Devon coastline. The Midlands contain high density urban sprawls that are surrounded by the beautiful limestone gorges of the Peak District and high,

open tracts of land. Miles of dry-stone walls criss-cross the landscape, keeping in the livestock. The hillsides are densely wooded and the roads are very often tree lined.

Moving east we come to the counties of Lincolnshire, Nottinghamshire, Norfolk and Suffolk, and then down to Essex, which leads into the great urban sprawl of London. Lincolnshire is famous for its flat, open tracts of land but we mustn't forget the hills of the Lincolnshire Wolds. Nottinghamshire has a history of coal mining and of course Sherwood Forest and its famous oak. Norfolk is famous for its Broads, and Norfolk and Suffolk together are renowned for their 'big skies', also known as 'Constable Skies'.

NORTHERN ENGLAND

Heading towards the north-west we come to the Lake District, which has been described as a 'mini Scotland' with its fells (mountains) and its many lakes and rivers lined with all the common types of trees from great oaks to hawthorns. There are many dry-stone walls, which vary in style from north to south in this area.

Like Wales this is a very wet area, but moving east over the Pennines and Cheviot Hills it becomes less so with more rounded hills and again dry-stone walls. On the levels towards the North Sea there are flatter and

With its deep limestone gorges and valleys, the Peak District of Derbyshire exhibits a special beauty.

The Lake District has a unique beauty aided by fantastic light, making it a magnet for artists.

The wide open expanse of the Yorkshire Dales is evident in this view, with dry-stone walls breaking up the landscape. The verdant dale bottom and the barrenness of its tops is very typical of this region.

more verdant areas where cereals are grown and hedgerows predominate. These plains give way to long stretches of sandy coastline, particularly to the north of Newcastle. As we move down towards Yorkshire the coastline gets craggier and we have the North York moors, which is a barren, heather-covered landscape. This gives way to the beautiful Yorkshire Dales with their wealth of dry-stone walls separating the livestock in a massive patchwork quilt of individual fields. Trees such as sessile and pedunculate oaks, ash, hazel and sycamore are very common.

WALES

This is a very wet area, but differs greatly from north to south. In the north lies the mountainous region of Snowdonia, with its proliferation of slate mines and narrow-gauge railways lying amongst terrain that varies from rocky outcrops to deep wooded valleys. Here you will find the more compact tree varieties, with oaks, wych elms, hawthorns and birch being the most common. South Wales has the Brecon Beacons, which lead into once heavily industrialized valleys that are now more wooded with the decline of coal and steel production. And all around it, Wales boasts a spectacular coastline.

SCOTLAND

Starting with the Borders, like Northumberland this region has a rolling landscape with farming of cattle and cereals. Trees in this region include crack willows, wych elms and oaks, but rowans are now starting to be more common. Moving on to the central lowlands, this area is heavily populated but also boasts grassy slopes, lochs and mountains with the broad plains populated by large urban sprawls. The industry in these areas has now diminished and Mother Nature is creeping back in again. Trees such as oaks and ashes, aspens, birches and alders are starting to be more common, along with the Scots pine or Caledonian pine.

The further north we move, the more mountainous and rocky the landscape becomes with deep lochs and barren mountains overlooking heavily wooded glens. Remnants of the Caledonian Forest are now regenerating, containing mostly Scots pine bordered by birches.

On the west coast areas such as the Ardnamurchan Peninsula carry some of the most ancient oak woods in the British Isles.

I will conclude this chapter by saying that there is nowhere in the world that carries such diverse and limitless landscape in such a small area as the British Isles.

ABOVE LEFT & RIGHT: Ancient Scottish woodland, with old oaks vying for the best position with lesser specimens, and with a carpet of bracken just starting to bud. Some of the ancient woodlands will have bluebells spread across the ground; this is very evident in May and will add even more interest when modelling such areas.

BELOW LEFT: 'Lonesome pine' in the Highlands of Scotland, where there was a massive clearance of the land a couple of centuries ago. Vast tracts of land were deforested to allow for sheep farming, and only the last vestiges of a great forest can still be seen. Luckily this is now being reversed by groups such as Trees For Life, which fence off large enclosures and allow the young sapling Scots pines to grow without deer nibbling off the tender shoots.

BELOW: Scotland offers a wide and varied landscape, with this west coast view showing a rugged, spectacular landscape. Within this formation there lie beautiful wooded glens populated with ancient oaks and silver birches.

CHAPTER ONE

STARTING OUT

The first thing you will need is a baseboard on which to place your railway and scenery. There are many different types, but the open-frame method seems to work the best. This is best described as a series of struts glued and screwed together to form an open, horizontal framework. Height above and below the track level can therefore be easily accomplished.

RIGHT: The glue gun comes in many shapes and sizes, but the best are those with a stand and a trigger feed for the glue stick. If you have one that has a thumb-push feed, then any significant amount of gluing will give you a pain in thumb, and the control is less user-friendly. The glue sticks are the general-purpose type, 10mm in diameter.

BELOW RIGHT: Artex is a trade name for air-drying decorative plaster. It dries more slowly than wall plaster such as Polyfilla and similar hole and crack fillers, though the drying time of these can be retarded by mixing in some PVA glue added to water. Colour is added to the decorative plaster in the form of powder paint. All the dry powders are mixed in an empty clear plastic container.

BELOW: A selection of palette knives and, in front, a plasterer's small tool. The palette knives are used to form the landscape substructures, while the wooden coffee stirrers are used for stirring paints and decorative plaster.

The traditional, flat baseboards can only give two dimensions – width and height – convincingly without recourse to major cutting and sculpting of the flat surface. Even the flattest of surfaces on the Earth have small undulations and it would seem that baseboards should be built with the Earth's surface in mind. But before rushing into building baseboards with a slight horizontal curve in them (mimicking the Earth's curvature), take a good look around and see how the landscape is formed. Make a sketch or take a few photographs, and then perhaps make a small mock-up to help get a good idea of how the model is to look.

FORMING THE SUBSOIL

Once the baseboards have been constructed, the subsoil can be started. There are several ways of achieving this; my favoured systems are hard shell and (discussed under 'Solid Landscape Form' later in this chapter) carved polyurethane foam board and stacked insulation board. Although there are other methods, these lend themselves best to our particular hobby. Long gone are the days of using chicken wire and papier mâché (very messy): this system leads to heavy baseboards, and chicken wire can be particularly vicious when it is cut. It will depend on the type of landscape that is to be represented as to which method is best to use.

Chicken wire fixed to plywood formers with the aid of staples is an altogether rather heavy and unwieldy construction, which needs a heavy baseboard.

HARD SHELL PROFILES

Hard shell profiles are used to make the shape of our landscape by supporting either an aluminium mesh or a basket weave of card. Begin to build above and below the track bed using these profiles. Should there be a vast area of track work such as a marshalling yard, then that is a straightforward, flat baseboard, but even here with a bit of forethought you could have a small, landscaped area at the front and back to add some interest in the scene. Provision should also made for the back scene to be fitted.

At the planning stage, work out how much of the landscape is raised above and below the track bed and allow some 150–225mm (6–9in) between landscape profiles. You should also consider what else is to be included in the landscape in the way of rivers, ponds, lakes, canals, bridge and so on. Sometimes when the baseboards have already been installed it is a little trickier to add height above and below the track level, so the process will have to be adjusted.

The profiles can be cut from any reasonably strong material: twin-walled corrugated card (cardboard boxes opened out and flattened), foam board, medium-density fibreboard (MDF) or high-density foam.

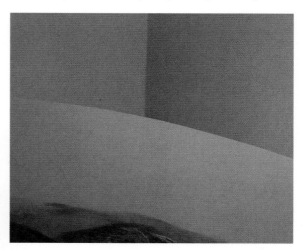

This is where some forethought comes into play: the back scene has been carried around a corner in an arc, cutting out that awkward right-angled corner that would otherwise be difficult to disguise. The ground work is then carried up the board to blend into the scene, giving a seamless transition.

The landscape profiles in this instance have been formed using foam board and have been set in place about 225mm (8¾in) apart. They are fixed to the baseboard using the hot-melt glue.

Now most of the profiles are in place and some of the 'mod mesh' has been glued to the top edge of the profiles.

Thin plywood profiles have been set in place and are integrated with the back board. This board has cut-outs in it to allow access to the void and to allow air to circulate, which in turn aids the drying process.

Profiles made from styrene board are best cut either with a jigsaw or, as here, by a bandsaw, but a small padsaw will also do the job.

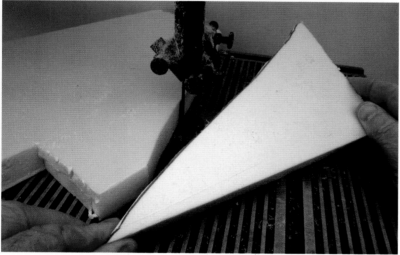

These profiles are then stuck to the baseboard with a building adhesive – preferably a non-solvent-based product, as this will not attack the profiles.

They are cut in such a way so as to give shape and form to the landscape. If the profiles are to be cut out of card, use a sharp modelling knife, being careful to keep fingers behind the blade. For plywood or MDF, which are usually 3–4mm thick, or the superlight 'styrene insulation board' (25mm thick), a jigsaw or bandsaw is used. All of these lightweight profile boards are fixed with hot-melt glue, PVA or panel adhesive – this last item comes in a tube similar to silicone sealant and is applied using a skeleton gun.

If a flat baseboard is in use, the profiles are held onto the baseboard with corner blocks or vertical supports. They are set on to the base of the landscape profile with

glue and screws if they are made of plywood or MDF, but are glued only if they are of card or foam board.

If everything has been planned correctly, everything, including the back scene, can be built in as part of the whole structure. Once the profiles have been positioned, then proceed to add either woven strips of card or Mod Mesh, as described below.

WOVEN CARD (ALSO CALLED A MATRIX)

Use card from cereal packets and similar types of cardboard packaging; never use corrugated card, for reasons that will become evident. Cut the card into strips 15mm (½in) wide and tack them horizontally with hot-melt glue over the profiles, leaving a gap of approximately 15–20mm (½–¾in) between each one. If the strips are not long enough to reach between two profiles just tack-glue them together, being careful not to burn your fingers while pinching the two pieces together. A quick-drying glue such as UHU can be used, or PVA, but this takes a little longer to go off: high-grab glues such as Speed Bond by Deluxe are useful. Once the horizontals are finished the vertical strips can be woven between the horizontals, again leaving a gap of 15–20mm between each vertical. This is what I call the matrix.

ADDING THE TISSUE

When the matrix is complete, proceed to glue tissue over the matrix. The tissue recommended for this process is the twin-ply type, which is used commercially and is purchased in rolls from commercial cleaning supply companies. It is also possible to use good quality newsprint, whichever is available at the time. Paint the matrix with PVA mixed with water, approximately three parts glue to one part water, and place the tissue onto this matrix. Whilst this is still wet a thin coat of decorative plaster (see below) is carefully applied with a large artist's paint brush or a 32mm soft decorator's paint brush. Another layer of tissue is added whilst this is still wet. Carefully paint over the whole lot with the thinned plaster mix and then leave to dry off a little in a warm room. When it is very nearly dry another coat of the decorative plaster is applied, this time minus its glue. The whole model is then left to dry completely before continuing further.

It should be noted that the tissue will kink and sometimes tear. This is not a problem as repairs can be done by adding another piece of tissue over the tear. Kinks and creases will add to the natural look of the landscape. The tissue will sag in the gaps between the matrix, but as it dries so it becomes taut and forms a hard drum-like skin over the surface.

MIXING THE DECORATIVE PLASTER

Before gluing the tissue down to the matrix mix up a slurry of decorative plaster. This plaster is also known

1. Twin-walled tissue – which is found in workshops and on garage forecourts, and is available from any commercial cleaning supply company – is very strong and extremely versatile. Kitchen towel is less strong and tends to fall apart when subjected to copious amounts of water; nevertheless, it can be used with care. Good-quality news print is also a reasonable substitute.

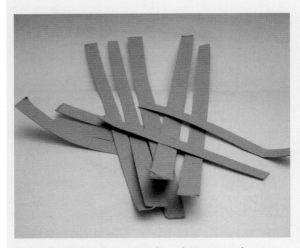

2. Cardboard such as cereal packets, tissue boxes and the like can be used for a matrix; it needs to be cut into strips about 15mm wide. Corrugated cardboard is not suitable for this.

3. The matrix is made by weaving the strips together with a gap between each strip equal to the width of the strips – about 15mm (½in).

ABOVE & RIGHT: 4. Weave the strips starting with the horizontals, which are attached to the profiles with use of a hot-melt glue gun. Then the verticals are slid in, weaving in and out until the whole area is covered.

continued overleaf

5. Paint the matrix with PVA (white wood-working glue).

6. Tissue is then pressed on to the wet glue, followed by a coat of fairly thin, pre-coloured decorative plaster, which is painted onto the tissue.

7. Then another layer of tissue is placed and pressed on to the wet plaster, followed by another coat of the mix.

8. The tissue will sag between the woven card strips but when the whole lot dries it will tighten and become like the skin on a drum.

by its trade name 'Artex'. It is an air-drying product and is usually white or off-white in colour, unlike wall plaster, which is a chemically drying product and is usually a pink colour. I once tried to use ordinary wall plaster, but found it to be too heavy and very quick-drying – too quickly to work easily – with a rather upsetting tendency to crack if a thick layer was added to the substructure. Adding PVA glue to the water helped to retard the setting time, but once it had dried it took a lot of work to obtain a good effect.

You should colour the plaster to match the underlying soil of the landscape being modelled: this way, if it is damaged at all the resultant chip or crack does not show up as an ugly white crack or chip. The powdered decorative plaster can be pre-coloured using powder paints, by adding 30–50ml (2–3 tablespoons) of colour per kilogram (2lb) of plaster. Put the dry powdered plaster in a plastic jar and add the colour (powder paint). Screw the lid on firmly and give the jar a good shake so that the plaster and powder paint will have mixed to a consistent colour throughout. The shade that has been mixed can be seen clearly. If it is too light, more colour pigment can be added. A question often asked at exhibitions is: 'When water is added to the mix the colour darkens dramatically, so will the finish stay that shade?' The answer is no: it will always dry back to the shade mixed when in powder form, or close to it. Always use clean water when mixing.

There is available a pre-mixed decorative plaster that comes in plastic tubs. Whilst this may have some benefits, it is difficult to add colour pigment to and therefore a consistent colour is hard to maintain.

Add a small amount of PVA or white woodworking glue to the first mix of decorative plaster, to help bond the tissue paper/newspaper to the structure. This PVA mix is for the first coat only and is mixed to a very thin consistency, something akin to single cream. It should be noted that when water is added to the mix the colour becomes very dark: as it dries it will lighten and become similar to the shade of the dry mixture.

1. A bag of Artex decorative plaster. There is a ready-mixed version, which should be avoided, as it is more expensive and is quite difficult to colour.

2. The decorative plaster and powder paint are mixed in an old, clear-plastic screw-lid container.

continued overleaf

3. *Powder paint is added to the decorative plaster. The amount you use depends on the subsoil or rocks' density of colour, but it is always better to aim for a slightly lighter shade, as a darker colour can be added at a later stage when all is dry.*

4. *Give the container a good shake to mix the two mediums together; as the container is a clear plastic, keeping a check on the mix is simple.*

5. *Tip a small amount of the pre-coloured plaster into a bowl (in this case a plastic pudding bowl), then add some PVA.*

6. *This is then mixed together and water is added, a little bit at a time, until a thin consistency is achieved: something akin to single cream.*

ALUMINIUM MESH (MOD MESH)

This mesh comes in rolls 3×0.5m (10ft×1ft 8in) wide, available in fine, medium and coarse gauge; I prefer to use the medium mesh, which has a 2mm square section – this makes it ideal when the 'soil' is applied. A strip of this mesh is cut and then fixed to the landscape profiles with a hot-melt glue gun. The mesh is very adaptable and useful, as it not springy and remains in shape once bent without any force. Unlike chicken wire, it doesn't cut the skin and is light in weight. The difficulty is in holding it down when used with lightweight landscape profiles.

Once the mesh is in place, mix the pre-coloured decorative plaster with water and a tiny drop of PVA, this time making sure the plaster mix is fairly thick in consistency. This is then spread over the supporting mesh with a plasterer's small tool or artist's palette knife. Be careful not to push so hard that the Artex squeezes through the mesh and drops to the floor: this takes a little practice but is worth persevering with. Alternatively, tissue can be applied to the Mod Mesh; it is glued down onto the mesh in a similar way to that described in the previous section.

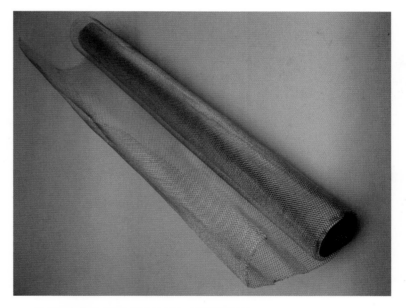

Aluminium mesh, also known as Mod Mesh, can be found in car repair kits, but it is only supplied in small amounts, making it quite expensive. A more economical solution is to buy a roll.

Chicken wire on heavy plywood formers has now been superseded by Mod Mesh.

The mesh is fixed to the formers with the hot-melt glue.
Be careful, as the glue and mesh can become hot.

A thicker mix of plaster is needed here as it is spread onto the mesh directly using the plasterer's small tool or a palette knife.

It should be spread with a light pressure...

...just enough to push the mix into the mesh, giving a key on the underside.

The Mod Mesh here has been treated with two layers of tissue as described earlier.

SOLID LANDSCAPE FORM

I use this method infrequently these days, but it is still viable when the low relief of a flat baseboard is the order of the day. There are two materials that I use for this method: insulation board (fibre board) and styrene board.

The insulation board can be broken up into strips or pieces and glued together to form an undulating landscape: this material is particularly useful when modelling low cuttings or forming low hills in the smaller scales. The sections are stacked on top of each other, much like a stack of plates but with each piece set back slightly from the edge of the piece below. This forms a contour of 9–12mm (½in) in height in each layer. It is quite a quick method with the use of PVA, but if a panel adhesive is used the process is even quicker – try to use the solvent-free type, as the fumes given off from the solvent-base type are quite unpleasant.

Polystyrene, although cheap and widely available, is messy and a lot more difficult to fix down. I do not like the stuff much, but when pushed have used vast amounts of it. Styrene board is much better. This takes adhesives of the non-solvent kind, is very easy to cut and sand, and must be the preferred medium after the insulation board.

A single piece of insulation board with the edge broken like this produces a reasonable representation of strata.

Here, insulation board is tacked and glued together with a setback on each layer to form a low embankment or cutting in the smaller scales.

All of the above systems can be covered with tissue and then decorative plaster, or directly with decorative plaster; the choice depends on the feature that we are trying to create.

Acrylic (water-soluble) panel adhesive is also known as building adhesive. There are also solvent-based adhesives, but they have quite a strong smell to them and are therefore not very user-friendly.

Styrene board is used in the building industry for insulation. It is dense with very good compressive strength, and comes in various colours and thicknesses.

CHAPTER TWO

CUTTINGS, CLIFF FACES AND ROCKY OUTCROPS

Sometimes we need to portray a railway running through a cutting or close to a river, or there may be a need for a ledge where the track runs around a mountain. These will inevitably require some exposed rock faces, which are a real challenge to get right; careful study of the subject is a definite necessity. As mentioned in the Introduction, it is important not to mix rock/strata from different areas if a realistic feel or look is to be achieved. There are products available commercially that represent rock faces, but these are unsatisfactory if realism is what you are after. The plastic moulds tend to be too repetitive, and though they offer different shapes and sizes, they will be of only one rock type; they will need a lot of work to make them convincing for, say, a limestone face. Such products have their place, but to create realistic rocky outcrops or steep cuttings it is generally better and much easier to model from scratch with decorative plaster.

Here a chalk cutting has been modelled complete with vegetation on the ledges. Note the staining to the right: this is a typical feature to be seen on chalk cliffs and when applied correctly adds realism to the scene. (This scene is on Peter Wiggins' O-gauge fine-scale layout, set in Southern England before nationalization.)

LANDSCAPE CUTTING AND CLIFF

MIXING THE PLASTER AND COLOUR PIGMENT

The mixing of decorative plaster is described in Chapter 1. The mix of plaster should be about the consistency of 'easy-spread' margarine: fairly thick, but not so thick that it cannot be spread easily. As a rough guide to the colouring process, two tablespoons (30ml) of colour should be added to 1lb (0.5kg) of plaster, but the precise amount will depend upon the depth of colour you want. Try to make the colour of the plaster mix a lighter shade than the soil of the prototype. Reflect the underlying colour/shade of the rock or soil of the countryside being modelled. Keep in mind that the soil may not be the same colour as the rock: for example, there is usually a brownish soil on top of a chalky cutting, so the underlying rock would be off-white and not brown.

APPLYING THE MIXED PLASTER

To begin the process, lightly thinned PVA glue is spread onto the surface of the pre-formed landscape, cutting or cliff. Make sure the area is of a size that can be comfortably covered with the plaster mix before the glue dries (*see box overleaf*).

It is not necessary to concern oneself with too much detail at this stage: spread the mix on with an artist's palette knife, with a 'general look' in mind. The detail on the face can be added later. It is preferable to have some moisture left on the surface when subsequent coats are applied. The next coat/mix that may be applied will 'flash set' if the undercoat has dried – this means the water in the mix will be sucked out very quickly, and the workability of the plaster is reduced dramatically.

Once the thick mix has been spread, take the palette knife and turn it so that the blade is horizontal. Start to drag the knife along the plaster, thus forming the strata. Stroke the plaster gently at first until you get a feel for the way it moves away from the knife. The plaster will drag (stick to the blade) more as drying takes place. To help with the drawing process, have a pot of clean water close by and dip the knife into this as necessary; this will make the plaster a little more workable. How the strata lie depends on the type of surface that is being modelled: limestone, for example, will look like lots of thin layers stacked on top of each other.

LEDGES AND PROJECTIONS

Where ledges are to be modelled, push the palette knife into the plaster while it is still wet, and gently push downwards. This will create a build-up of the mix under the bottom face of the tool. Next, slowly pull the knife out of the plaster. Tidy up the ledge with a small No.3 paint brush as the plaster dries.

Ledges can be made by pushing the palette knife into the plaster and then gently downwards, creating a build-up of plaster on the bottom edge of the blade. Carefully remove the tool and tidy up using a No.3 paint brush.

1. Paint the surface with a lightly thinned PVA.

2. The plaster mix is fairly thick to accommodate the Mod Mesh used to form the landscape. A little PVA is added to bond and to aid with the drying.

3. Spread the mix fairly generously over the ground. Do not worry about any detail yet: this can be applied as work progresses.

4. Once the thick mix has been spread over the surface, turn the palette knife so that the blade is horizontal and gently drag the edge along the plaster, forming the strata as you go.

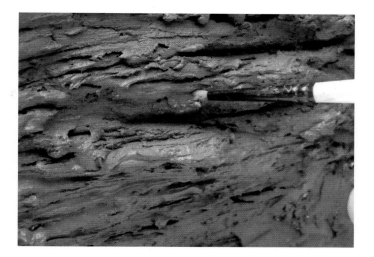

Detail can also be 'painted' in with a No.3 paint brush.

SLATE AND GRANITE

If a slate or granite rock face is to be modelled, turn the palette knife with its face flat against the plaster. Press this gently into the damp surface and pull the knife across the face so that a smooth finish is achieved. Turn the tool so that the edge or tip faces the plaster. Gently cut vertical or slightly angled fissures (cracks) to form sheets or slabs of rock.

Finally, when all is dry brush lightly over the surface with an old toothbrush. This takes of any 'nibs' or burrs that may form and will also age the finish.

MODELLING SLATE OR GRANITE

1. To replicate granite or slate, turn the palette knife flat against the wet mix and, with the leading edge, gently drag the knife along the surface to form a flat face.

continued overleaf

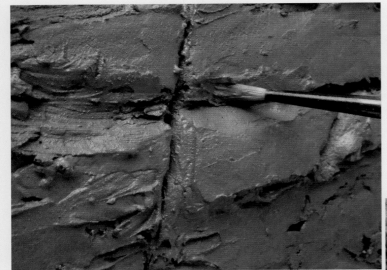

2. Tidy up and add small detail, again using the No.3 brush.

3. Leave to dry before brushing over the whole face using an old toothbrush; this will take of any unwanted nibs of dry plaster. Then paint using water-colours, finishing off with vegetation planted on the ledges.

MODELLING ROCKY OUTCROPS

So often seen, yet rarely modelled, rocky outcrops can add depth to an otherwise barren hillside (*see box overleaf*). They can be represented by gluing down loosely screwed-up newspaper, aluminium foil or tissue. Apply a neat coating of PVA to the underside of the chosen material, and press this into the previously glued landscape, making sure that the edges are well glued down. Paint a lightly thinned coat of PVA glue over the surface so that it is fully lapped onto the main surface of the landscape. Proceed to spread on a plaster mix that has just enough PVA added to aid the setting and bonding process; this will make the structure solid when dry. Add more plaster, this time without any additional PVA in the mix.

ADDING THE DETAIL

This is done with an artist's palette knife and either a fairly stiff paint brush or a No. 3 artist's brush. Use the palette knife to blend the landscape and rocky outcrop together. Next, gently drag the paint brush across the wet surface; as the plaster dries it will cling to the hairs of the brush, leaving a rough appearance. A few drops of water on a paint brush loaded with the plaster mix will give the same effect. The brush can also be used to paint and smooth detail into the mix. The decorative plaster is designed to have patterns drawn into it, so it is really flexible and allows for extra detail to be added. The versatility of this plaster will become evident in later chapters. Paying careful attention to the detailing at this stage will add to the realistic feel of the finished model. Short cuts will show up later, by which time it will probably be too late to alter.

COLOURING CUTTINGS AND ROCK FEATURES

After the work has dried the finish can be further enhanced by the use of water-colour paints (*see box on pp.36–8*). The use of water-colour is recommended as a more gentle change in shade and colour can be achieved. Always work with plenty of clean water to hand so that if any mistakes are made they can washed out. If there are any fissures or vertical cracks on the model, these can be made a more prominent feature.

Start by floating in a dark colour – something like black, dark grey or, in the case of chalk, dark brown/green. To do this, soak the dried plaster around the feature and then drop in the colour. As the water runs down, so the colour is taken with it, soaking into the plaster as it goes. Add more colour as it dries.

DRY BRUSHING

To further accentuate these details a method called dry brushing can be employed. Load a small (maybe No. 7) paint brush with white paint. Carefully remove most of the paint, leaving the brush almost dry. Pass the brush over the surface using a light flicking motion. Small amounts of paint will be deposited onto the high points, thus highlighting them.

ADDING MORE DETAIL

Detail such as water seeping through the rock face and trickling down can be added. This is achieved by carefully applying a high-gloss varnish or high-gloss acrylic paint. The first coat is painted on and will dry to a matt finish as it disappears into the plaster. This coat really acts as a primer and seals the plaster – it is subsequent coats that will show up. Carefully paint on the varnish, making sure that the 'flow' down the slope looks natural. Leave to dry in a warm room.

To accentuate features such as ledges, use lighter colours on top and darker underneath. It is better to experiment first. In most cases these ledges will have some form of vegetation on them, which can be applied after the 'wet work' is dry: more is said about this in following chapters.

CREATING A ROCKY OUTCROP

1. The real thing. This rocky outcrop is on the Isle of Mull and shows how vegetation will grow just about anywhere.

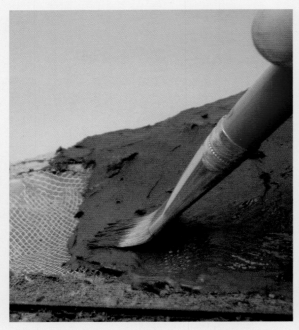

2. Paint a small amount of PVA onto the wet plaster before proceeding to the next stage.

3. A small piece of tissue is coated with PVA in readiness to being 'planted' into the wet plaster.

4. Work the 'planted' tissue's edges into the wet ground with some of the glue.

5. Paint the tissue all over with the slightly thinned plaster mix.

ABOVE LEFT & RIGHT: **6.** Liberally apply the thicker mix over the whole area. Detail can be added a little later.

1. Detailing can now be started with the aid of a paint brush.

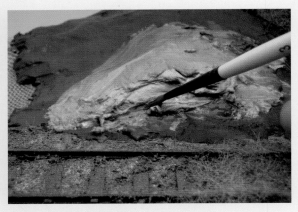

2. This plaster is designed to allow patterns to be drawn into it.

3. It is extremely useful for our purposes.

4. The colour of the plaster in this state is quite different to how it will end up once the water has evaporated. The outcrop should be left to dry a little before the next stage is attempted.

5. Drag an artist's palette knife carefully through the semi-dry plaster.

6. Detail begins to form.

7. As the plaster dries so the detail starts to emerge, and when the outcrop is completely dry painting can begin. This is always the most interesting part for it is only now that all your hard work starts to bear fruit.

8. A base colour is used here to embellish the outcrop.

9. Then the subsoil colour is added where necessary with the darker topsoil over this.

10. Staining by the subsoil can be represented by dry-brushing over the high spots with a rusty subsoil colour.

11. Any extra detail – such as, in this case, flint – can be painted in.

12. There is also room for a little ageing in the form of a light green, again dry-brushed to give even more depth of realism.

continued overleaf

13. The whole outcrop now looks a natural part of the landscape. How the whole scene is grassed over is covered in Chapter 3.

ABOVE LEFT & RIGHT: **This rocky outcrop is being created for my own model railway. It is part of a gorge that has a river running under a railway bridge similar to that in Millers Dale, Derbyshire, which was built by the Midland Railway in the 1800s. The rocks form a lead into the back scene and are some 600mm (24in) in height.**

RIGHT: **Water seeping through the rock face is represented by high-gloss oil-based varnish. The first coat is really only a primer coat to seal the porous plaster and can be a matt varnish.**

CHAPTER THREE

LET IT GROW: GRASS, VEGETATION, WATER MARGINALS AND FLOWERS

Grass and vegetation have always intrigued me, but in the many years I have spent exhibiting and visiting model railway shows this subject mostly seems to have been brushed aside. Though most modellers seem to give very little thought to the colours of grass and vegetation, it can make or break a good model: if it is bright and gaudy, the unrealistic effect created will distract the viewer from the rest of the model and turn them away.

All colours are a reflection of light. At first sight, a beautifully manicured lawn may look all one colour, but in fact there will be many shades of green ranging from yellowing to verdant. A hay field with young shoots will have fresh and vibrant colours, then in late spring/early summer many new colours and shades will start to show as the little swords began to grow. Bare soil will reflect a brownish shade onto the green, and the sun shining at an angle will create more colour differences; a cloud passing overhead will change the light and therefore the colour. Therefore a field or a patch of grass on a model will have to show several shades of green, and there should be subtle colour changes rather than drastic contrasting shades.

This very summery view shows a great mix of flowers and grass, with its many shades of green. Even in this small area there is a lighter colour to centre left and a darker green to the right (shadow from a tree), and in the middle distance an almost straw-like colour. The foliage on the trees is also worth noting.

Here is a small selection of some of the scatters that are used to create realism in our models.

In the last few years static fibres have become more popular. When they are used correctly they can really look the part.

It is best to exercise restraint on bright colours in all scales of modelling. The modern trend in Europe is towards huge fields of oilseed rape or linseed plants: these can make an attractive feature, but are very bright when in flower even on a dull day. In model form a 'letdown' in the intensity of the colour is necessary.

LETTING DOWN COLOURS

To 'let down' a colour means to reduce its intensity or brightness, and is achieved by adding a touch of white or black to the colour in question. Very small amounts will make quite a difference, so experiment to start with. (It is a little known but interesting fact that quite a high number of males over forty years of age have colour blindness of some kind. This affliction is apparently less common in females.)

GRASS

There are many mediums that can be used to represent grass: surgical lint, crumbed latex or cellulose,

This is a good candidate for static grass, as we will see. Again many shades of green show through, with the seed heads giving height to the grass at the edge of the field.

carpet underlay (of the 'hairy' kind), car sound-proofing, teddy bear fur, static fibres and commercially made grass matting. All of these have their place, but none exclusively.

SURGICAL LINT

Lint is of limited use, but it is very good at replicating a close-cut garden or meadow in the smaller scales.

Application

Cut a piece of lint oversize for the intended area – with the sheet being oversize, any errors made when sticking it down can be accommodated – and pre-colour the sheet using fabric dye. The time of year that is being modelled will have a bearing on the colour/shade chosen: if it is high summer, then an underlying straw colour will be used, onto which various greens can be applied. Remember to keep the colour/shade light or 'mute', and never use a green that has a blue tint to it. This would always look heavy and it is difficult to disguise once glued to the model. It is essential to leave the lint to dry before attempting the next stage.

Glue down the whole sheet, furry side up, using either carpet spray adhesive or PVA glue. Let it dry, then cut away the surplus lint. Next, nap up the fibres with an old toothbrush before passing a pair of electric clippers with a number I shear over the whole area to take off any over-height whiskers. A sharp pair of scissors will also do the job.

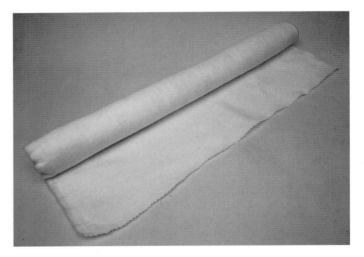

Surgical lint comes on rolls and in small packets. It is difficult to obtain and is also becoming expensive.

The lint is coloured with either dye or paint. The base coat colour depends on the time of year being modelled.

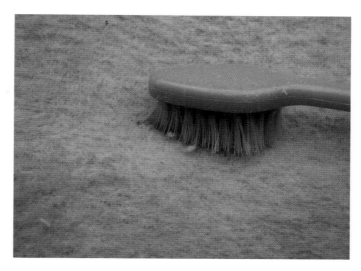

The surface can be 'napped' with an old toothbrush. A burnishing brush can also be used, but care must be taken to avoid tearing into the lint and damaging it.

Small amounts of scatter are sprinkled onto a lightly sprayed coat of hair spray. More colour is then added to the 'grass' in the form of water-colour paint applied with a No.3 artist's brush or sprayed with an airbrush. The whole area is then dried with the aid of a hairdryer.

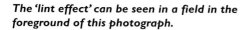

The 'lint effect' can be seen in a field in the foreground of this photograph.

The straw colour is used to represent dead grass, but spring grass is different again: it is all down to observation and translating this correctly to give the model a realistic feel. To add a 'natural height' to the lint, add back the clipped fibres; these can be placed around the edge of a field or garden, using a very tacky hair spray to hold them in place. Alternatively, a very fine scatter material – either crumbed latex or cellulose – can be used. The whole lot is fixed with a final coat of either hair spray or a well-watered-down matte medium.

LATEX AND CELLULOSE CRUMB

This is a very popular medium, and rightly so as it is so very versatile. Latex crumb comes in fine, medium and coarse grades; the cellulose comes in similar grades but with an added coarse texture or 'clumping' grade that is useful for hedges and small shrubs (more of which in the following chapters). An even finer grade can be obtained by sieving the latex crumb through a flour sieve: this fine crumb is especially useful in the smaller scales.

Application

Spread a neat and even layer of PVA glue or carpet adhesive over the landscape surface, and allow it to become tacky. Spread the crumb over the surface with a sieve, gently tapping the side. A fine rain of scatter will settle on the glue. Whilst this is still wet, add some coarser scatter where necessary. Spray over the top with either hair spray or matte medium.

To go one step further, more of the finer scatter may be sprinkled over the already-laid coarse crumb. Then perhaps some colour to represent either gorse or wild roses.

CARPET UNDERLAY/ CAR SOUND-PROOFING

Hairy carpet underlay/car sound-proofing is used to represent grass and, when worked in with latex crumb and static fibres, gives a very good representation of wild grass. It has become rare and the new types that are appearing have a lot of 'lumpy bits' added to bulk it up, so there are less fibres to represent blades of grass.

Application

Take a square of the material 150×150m (6×6in) and carefully delaminate it: several thinner sheets can be taken out of the original thickness. There is a reinforcing matrix in the centre that must be removed.

There are two ways of using these thinned squares. One is to stick down a delaminated sheet using carpet

Latex and cellulose scatter or crumb are very popular mediums. They are made in grades ranging from fine to very coarse, or 'clumping', grade.

A much finer crumb is extracted by sieving a medium/coarse latex scatter. This fine crumb is extremely useful in the smaller scales.

Applying latex/cellulose crumb

1. Spread a bed of neat PVA (or white woodworking) glue over the landscaped surface, a small area at a time. If using carpet spray glue, then a larger area can be covered, but it is best to let this go tacky before any scatter is applied – it will take about a minute. As this glue is solvent based, plenty of ventilation is required.

2. Sprinkle on the scatter and leave it to dry a little, then tap and brush away any of the crumb that has not adhered to the surface. Do not throw the surplus away but collect it up and reuse it on the next section.

3. Now we have a good base onto which detail can be added.

4. By spraying the base coat of scatter with hair spray or a matte medium, a coarser crumb/scatter can be added, giving depth to the scene.

1. Hairy carpet underlay is becoming very scarce. If you can find some, make sure it is of a buff/beige colour. Dark brown underlay can be bleached, but the bleach must be fully washed out and dried before it is used.

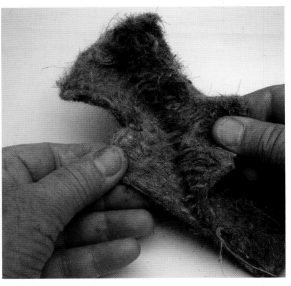

2. Carefully delaminate the underlay so there are about three or four thin sheets.

3. Discard the reinforcing matrix in the centre.

4. Depending on which method you are using, cut the delaminated underlay into squares or thin strips.

spray adhesive, allowing it to become tacky before the square is pressed on. Pull the sheet off again, leaving tufts attached to the model. Be very careful here as you may inadvertently pull off the substructure. When an area has been covered in this way, use hair clippers or scissors to trim any wayward tufts, as described in the previous section.

Apply a coat of light green paint sprayed over the whole area: this should be a water-based colour, as most of the fibres are natural. The colour pigment will be soaked up, leaving subtle shades of green and straw that can be added to, to give more depth. Acrylic spray paint can be used, but although it works quite well the fibres become crisp when dry, making them a little more difficult to work.

The second method involves cutting up the delaminated underlay into small strips approximately 6–9mm (¼–⅜in) wide, depending on whether the grass to be modelled is a rough piece of land or of a more level, playing field type. The smaller or narrower the strips, the more work that will be needed to cover a given surface.

With this system always use water-resistant PVA glue. The reasoning behind this is that the fibres are going to be shaded with water colours, which might reactivate non-water-resistant glues. This creates a matted mess of the fibres, which are forced down into the glue, never to rise again.

Spread the PVA glue over an area 150mm (6in) square. Take a strip and push the end into the wet glue. With a pair of cranked tweezers or a small wooden spatula (the coffee-stirrer sort), hold the strip down in the glue. Pull the remainder away, leaving a tuft of grass in the glue. Move quickly, repeating the whole procedure until the glued area is covered.

The Long and the Short

Trim any unwanted grass tufts to length. Remove any loose grass and fill in any gaps with shorter tufts. Finally, tidy up with the clippers or scissors.

This particular method holds another useful side: it enables grass to be added to rocky ledges on cliffs, cuttings, old buildings, walls and so on. By dabbing the surface with a drop of glue, the tufts can be planted at will.

USING CARPET UNDERLAY

1. Spread some water-resistant glue over an area about 75mm (3in) square. Next, press the end of one of the strips into the glue and, holding it there with a suitable tool (in this case a pair of cranked tweezers), pull the strip away, leaving a tuft implanted in the glue. Continue like this until the whole area is covered.

continued overleaf

2. *Doing small squares at a time makes the work easier to control, and the glue remains usable.*

3. *Water-colour paint is used to colour the grass, giving a subtle shade of green when dry that allows a more natural look to the finish. Other shades can be added as one sees fit, to enhance the look even further.*

4. *The flattened tufts, once dry, can be teased up with a toothbrush. Note that if the glue is not water-resistant, then the glue will reactivate when the water paint is applied: the whole area will become a matted mess, making it almost impossible to recover a grass-like look.*

The carpet underlay method allows small detail to be added to models, be it a ledge on a cliff face, the base of a building or boundary wall, or between the rails of a little-used track. This model is Peter Wiggins' O Gauge pre-nationalization Southern Railway.

These tufts are best left in their natural state, beige or straw-coloured. Just a hint of green paint can be added in strategic places, topped with a pinch of scatter. The whole lot should then be held in place with a quick squirt of tacky hair spray.

STATIC FIBRES

These fibres come in various sizes from 2–6.5mm (1/12–1/4in) in length and are made from nylon. Some manufacturers produce a very shiny fibre whilst others have more of a satin finish. The fibres, when charged with static electricity, will separate from each other. When applied to a bed of PVA glue or a similar adhesive, the single strands will stand erect. I originally applied static fibres with the help of a puffer bottle:

Static fibres range in sizes from 2mm to 6.5mm in length and are a very attractive proposition for landscape modelling.

this is alright for small areas, but if you use a static generator instead, the results that can be obtained are quite amazing.

A Natural-Looking Colour Mix

To obtain the best effect, use a mixture of approximately 75 per cent beige/straw and 25 per cent mid-green: the beige/straw represents dead grass and the mid-green fresh young shoots. This will give a good foundation on to which a realistic finish can be built. Sometimes the beige/straw colour is more useful on its own, adding small splashes of green where necessary to represent high summer or winter.

Puffer Bottle Method

This is a plastic bottle with a removable perforated cap. The bottle is similar to a pepper pot but with much larger holes.

Begin by spreading a coat of lightly thinned PVA glue over the chosen area. Place the fibres in the puffer bottle until it is about one-third full. Puff out the fibres by squeezing the bottle quickly and firmly, holding it about 50mm (2in) from the glue. The fibres will be charged with static electricity as they pass through the holes in the cap, so they will head, spear-like, into the glue. When the glue is dry an overspray of adhesive (hair spray) will allow a further application of a slightly different shade of green to be added.

Static Generator Method

The 'Noch Grassmaster' is a combination of electronic wizardry that puts a static charge into the coloured nylon fibres. A choice of two sieves – fine and coarse – is available, the fine sieve being for the shorter lengths of fibres and the coarse sieve for the longer ones. There is also a cone supplied with a choice of two inserts; this directs the fibres to a smaller area when the generator is used in restricted areas.

Static generators are easy to use and to clean. They are expensive but, when covering large or small areas with static fibres, they are invaluable. The method of application is similar to the puffer bottle, but larger areas can be grassed more quickly.

ABOVE & BELOW: 1. A puffer bottle is very good for getting into small areas. About a third of the bottle is loaded with the fibres, and with a few snappy squeezes the fibres fly out through the lid, charged with static electricity.

2. Not all of the fibres stand up when the puffer bottle is used. To overcome this overspray with hairspray and puff on further fibres, and finally fix with another spraying of hairspray.

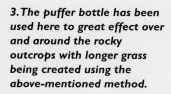

3. The puffer bottle has been used here to great effect over and around the rocky outcrops with longer grass being created using the above-mentioned method.

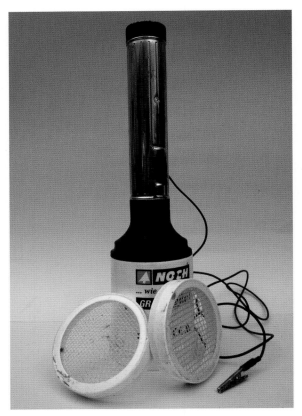

This static generator is a superb piece of modelling equipment. There are quite a few plans for home-made versions on the internet but this purpose-made model is the best bet.

Spread lightly thinned glue to an area of approximately 300×300mm (12×12in). The glue may dry quite quickly in a warm atmosphere, so this is about the largest area that can be managed at any one time. There is a ground wire, which is attached to a brass screw or long panel pin and pushed into the landscape somewhere nearby on the model. The landscape does not have to be electrically conductive. It is preferable to dampen the area around the previously glued landscape, as this will aid the statically charged fibres. Half-fill the container with the chosen length of coloured fibre mix, and you are ready to begin.

Switch the static generator on and, holding it about 50mm (2in) from the surface, gently tap or shake the unit. The fibres will shoot out through the sieve and land upright in the glue. Continue to move across the glued area in circular movements until all of the glue is covered. Move on to the next patch and do the same again. Once that area is complete move back to the start and spray across the surface with a hair spray. Allow the spray to dust the top of the upright fibres, but don't soak the upright fibres to heavily. Then apply another coat of fibres, varying the colours as necessary.

Further detail can be added by another application of hair spray. With the aid of a fine flour sieve, lightly dust small areas with fine crumb: this will give the effect of taller plants within the grass.

Some of the static fibres available.

The static generator will help give a fairly accurate representation of terrain such as this.

APPLYING STATIC FIBRES WITH A STATIC GENERATOR

1. Spread lightly thinned P.V.A. to an area of approximately 300×300mm (12×12in). The glue may dry quite quickly in a warm atmosphere so this is about the largest area that can be managed at any one time.

continued overleaf

2. Attach the ground wire to the model and spray the area with some water. This helps the statically charged fibres to stand erect in the glue. Then switch on the generator after filling the container to about one-third full. Screw on the mesh grill and begin to apply the grass using small, circular movements, keeping the applicator approximately 50mm (2in) away from the glued surface.

3. To add more fibres lightly spray across the top of the 'grass' with hairspray and apply more fibres.

4. Carefully sweep up any unfixed fibres to be re-used.

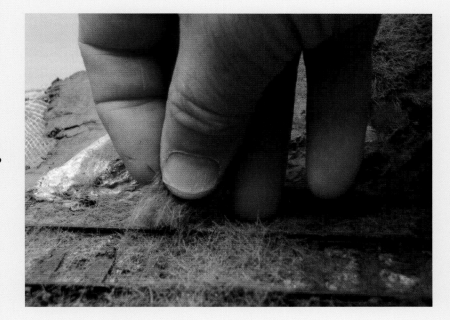

5. With care, some fibres can be added to a spot of glue, to represent tufts of grass.

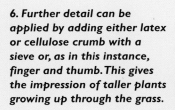

6. Further detail can be applied by adding either latex or cellulose crumb with a sieve or, as in this instance, finger and thumb. This gives the impression of taller plants growing up through the grass.

THE END RESULT

The static grass used here along with the latex/cellulose crumb gives a good representation of summer grass in a woody environment. This particular model is to be used to fill an awkward corner of a large layout in 4mm (OO) gauge.

TEDDY BEAR FUR FABRIC

Teddy bear fabric comes in various shades from blonde to dark brown, though I would suggest using a colour somewhere in between those extremes, for example a golden brown. This can be used for small patches of long grass or areas of longer grass.

Application

Spray the ground with carpet glue or spread neat PVA evenly over the surface. Cut the fabric a little larger than the area that is to be covered, press the sheet into the glue and leave to dry (see box opposite).

Be vigilant when joining sheets together: a staggered joint is much more preferable than a straight one. Once this has been accomplished, use clippers to trim the height as described earlier, making random passes. Then a dusting with various shades of green paint will be necessary; follow this with a liberal coating of hair spray and a few crumbs of scatter to add interest.

COMMERCIALLY MADE GRASS MATTING

Paper-backed grass matting, although very popular, is not of use to us as it tends to be too regular, too gaudy and not very realistic. Fibrous matting such as Mini-Natur or Silflor, on the other hand, can be very useful, particularly in small areas. It comes in small mats and in many shades with varying lengths of fibres. It is very adaptable as the way it is manufactured

Teddy bear fabric comes in many colours, but the golden brown is by far the most useful colour. I have found it to be very useful for small areas in the scales of 3.5mm HO, 4mm OO and 7mm O.

allows for cutting into small pieces. This can be useful when 'planting' grass between the rails, on a path or around the edge of a building.

The whole mat can be glued down with either carpet spray adhesive or a thin layer of PVA. Detail can then be added with a light spraying of hair spray and a small pinch of a fine latex/cellulose crumb; this will break the monotony of colour and give some height. There are also many types of self-adhesive grass tufts that come on a polythene sheet. These are useful in areas such as abandoned or neglected buildings, railway yards and track work, along the base of retaining walls and so on. Pick them off with a pair of tweezers and – as a 'belt and braces' measure – dab the base with a spot of glue and press home in the chosen spot.

FLOWERS

Whether we are representing spring, summer, autumn or winter on our models, there are flowers for all seasons. Many modellers overdo bright colours: whilst there are fields of poppies, blue linseed along with the yellow of oilseed rape, these will look better if they are understated on the model. With just a suggestion of colour the brain will do the rest.

Colourful flowers are an important part of the scene. In a boggy patch at the bottom of an embankment, reeds will often grow, bearing small, white flowers. Around the edges of ponds or streams plants such as marsh marigolds, which have bright yellow flowers from March to July, will grow. If the model is in a chalk area, then specific plants will grow in abundance. A chalk stream will have such plants as chalk stream water crowfoot, which is a white flower with a yellow centre (difficult to model in a smaller scale) flowering from May to September. A good all-rounder to add height to a pond or a slow-running stream is the yellow iris, which flowers from May to August.

Moving into the grasslands and open countryside, common ragwort is to be seen from June through to November; it can be quite tall, about 1m (3ft) with yellow flowers. Yarrow will be found on the wayside and stands approximately 1m (3ft) in height with white flowers and black tops, appearing in the months from June to November.

APPLYING TEDDY BEAR FABRIC

1. Once the fabric is glued down (usually in small sheets) the fibres are brushed up and given a light dusting of hair spray.

2. These electric hair clippers are a very useful aid in creating natural-looking grass.

3. Clipping the fabric carefully and in a random fashion produces good effects.

4. Once the desired height has been reached, your chosen colours can be sprayed over the top. Do this a little at a time, letting the spray paint dry between coats. Once you are happy with the colour, then a liberal coating of hair spray can be added along with a few crumbs of scatter to add interest.

Poppies are very bright when massed together in a field and viewed from a distance, but when looked at closer are fairly well spread out and less bright.

Seen widely across the land, rose bay willow herb and purple loosestrife stands up to 1.2m (4ft) in height and favours waste ground, river banks and railway embankments; it is very recognizable by its pinkish/purple flower stems.

MODELLING THE FLOWERS

This method for making flowers and plants tends to work better in the larger scales. When modelling the taller plants, materials such as brush bristles, sisal string and cartridge paper are very useful.

This overgrown and disused railway is full of the sort of wild flowers that can enhance any model.

On this close-up several ferns can be seen, along with various wild flowers including the yellow flower of the mouse-ear hawkweed (a very common plant and member of the daisy family). When modelled, these flowers should be sparse: this allows the brain to imagine there are more and, as a result, the scene is brought to life.

Thoughtful positioning of any tall wild flower will add to the illusion.

Tall Plants

Pick out two or three pieces of brush bristle, dip the ends in PVA glue or spray them lightly with spray glue, and gently roll them in a carefully chosen coloured scatter (see box overleaf). Use a green to start, closely followed by the flower colour; a gentle tap of the stems will remove any excess. This method works very well for rose bay willow herb and purple loosestrife. For yarrow, start in the same manner but use a mid-green scatter as the undercoat. After this has dried, the end of the bristle is dipped into PVA glue and then into a white scatter.

Bunch three or five pieces together – odd numbers look more convincing together than even numbers. This simple rule applies to every part of scenic modelling where groups of trees, plants and flowers are to be seen.

Yellow Iris

These are made with cartridge paper for the leaves, with a bristle or fine copper wire for the flower stem; this is then topped with a yellow scatter (see box on p.63). To make the leaves, colour the cartridge paper using watercolour paint and draw on elongated arrow heads. Carefully cut the leaves with a craft knife or scalpel. Each leaf can have a small curl put on the end: to do this, pinch two cocktail sticks together, pass the leaf through the sticks bringing the leading end back towards the cocktail sticks. Straighten the bottom end between the fingers. Collect several of these together with a tall flower stem in the middle and add a touch of PVA glue. Roll the base of the plant between the thumb and forefinger. Set aside and leave to dry before planting.

There is on the market a product by the Dutch company Anita-Decor called Cactus Plants: these are seed heads that can be altered to great effect. Pick off any unwanted fine hairs, spray the tips of the 'leaves' with a suitable adhesive (hair spray) and dip the ends in a yellow scatter. Give the whole plant a final coat of matt varnish or matte medium, and leave to dry.

Carpet Tuft Flowers

Flowers can be made from tufted green carpet samples, which can be obtained from carpet shops. Be especially careful to make sure that the pile is tufted and not looped. The tufts are very good for the representation of small plants in areas such as garden borders, station planters and rock ledges. The tufts can also 'planted' between tracks in a disused part of a siding.

Cut off a small square of the carpet, strip off all of the backing to expose the web/matrix of the carpet sample. With a pair of tweezers pluck individual tufts from the weave before spraying them with tacky hair

MODELLING TALL PLANTS

1. The bristle is either sprayed or dipped in glue.

2. Next, it is rolled in the scatter material. A gentle tap will remove any loose scatter.

3. By shortening the stem/bristle a little, plants like ragwort can be represented.

4. Make a small hole in the landscape and dip the stems/bristles into some PVA. Carefully 'plant' the stems/bristles, remembering to keep these groups in odd numbers.

Carpet tufts plucked from a carpet sample and treated with a spray of adhesive (hair spray), then dipped into a coloured scatter will create a good likeness to plants such as rose bushes, daffodils or even buttercups.

1. Some of the cartridge paper leaves are curled at the top, but not all of them.

2. Place the flower stems in the middle of the group and fix with PVA. This is achieved by rolling the base of the plant between the thumb and forefinger.

3. 'Cactus' from Anita-Decor used to great effect to represent yellow iris close to water. Note that in this model not enough of the fine hairs have been removed.

spray. Then dip the coated fibres in coloured scatter; give the tuft a gentle tap to remove any surplus scatter before gluing into place using a touch of PVA glue.

MARGINALS AND WATERSIDE PLANTS

Bulrushes, reeds and the like can be made from various materials, both artificial and natural. These plants generally grow close to or in water, and around the margins of ponds streams or rivers. They are relatively easy to make.

Reeds

Reeds can be made from small tufts of sisal. A good old brush bristle is better than sisal that has been twisted into rope or string. Brush manufacturers tend to use acrylic bristle nowadays, but natural products are sold by model landscape material suppliers.

Cut off a length of sisal and form a small bundle, then dip the end of the bunch into PVA glue. Roll this lightly between thumb and forefinger so that the glue forms a solid plug. To make two clumps in one go, dab the middle of a slightly longer bundle of bristles into PVA glue.

A typical pond scene with numerous marginal plants. In fact there is so much detail here it would make a standalone project/diorama.

MODELLING REEDS

1. Cut a small bunch of sisal (as here) or a similar straight material to length.

2. Dab the end of the small bunch with PVA glue.

3. Roll the glue-laden sisal between the thumb and forefinger. This will form a plug of glue once it has dried.

4. Trim the plant to the required length.

5. If making small water-side flowering plants, then a blob of glue can be applied to represent the flower heads.

6. The stems are carefully painted and colour added to the flower head.

7. When there is a group of plants there is no need to add a flower head to all the stems.

Roll this between the thumb and forefinger in similar manner to before. Let the glue dry before cutting through the middle of the glue to give two clumps.

Colour is then applied using either Indian ink or water-colour paint.

Bulrush

The bulrush is slightly different as it is relatively tall, and each seed head needs to be made individually. Lay each strand of sisal on a sheet of polythene and pre-colour by dragging the paint brush loaded with Indian ink along the strand. Alternatively, use a felt-tip pen — fiddly, but worth the effort. The end is then dipped into a small pot of heavy-structure gel, or PVA glue. A small blob (or 'seed head') will form; let this dry before colouring with a dab of paint. The gel will give a better build-up, but it will have to be painted carefully with a fine paint brush. The leaves are not dissimilar to the iris and are much shorter than the seed head; the seed head can rise in height up to 2m (6ft+) and, if modelled correctly, will look really authentic when planted.

Marsh Marigolds

These can be made as described in the section describing carpet tufts for flowers.

A bulrush ready to plant; it will take many of these to make a real impact.

CHAPTER FOUR

WATER

This is without doubt the most difficult thing to model convincingly, but it is to my mind an essential part of any model railway. The railway engineers of yesteryear had to do battle with rivers, lakes and even small, unassuming streams, for even these could undermine all their hard work. A vast amount of planning was needed and, in some cases, massive deviations either of the route the railway took or of the river line. Railways very often ran alongside the canals that were their forerunners in Great Britain and most of Europe. All railway yards, stations and depots had to be drained, so there would be a culvert leading to a stream, river or pond. There would always be water somewhere close at hand, unless you are modelling a desert railway – and even then you might come across an oasis! A viaduct over a river valley is a lovely feature, a canal basin alongside an industrial scene always creates interest, and so on.

ABOVE: 'Just a moment to reflect.' This scene won't be seen on many layouts.

LEFT: This picture was taken for a survey on a project called Great Elm. It shows the value of research when it comes to getting the model right.

If modelled well, a stream or river running over rocks will be a very attractive feature whilst a calm pond with a willow beside will reflect the scene all around. Ripples where a breeze has hit the surface will add an incalculable dimension for the viewer. If the water is clear, then underwater features give a realism that will allow the mind to wander further into the scene.

However, real water on a layout will not look right. Waves or ripples will not be to scale and 'angry water' will be almost impossible to create. The model would need to be waterproofed and sealing any joints between baseboards would be extremely difficult.

LAKES, PONDS AND RIVERS

These features will all need a good bed in which to lie and to a great degree are the most important part of

the whole natural scene. Therefore, time spent 'getting it right' here will be time well spent. Making sure that the bed is level and true is very important: if it is not, it will look unconvincing. To achieve the perfect finish, make sure the bed has a flat platform.

FORMING THE POND, LAKE OR RIVER BED

Timber and Particle Board

Start by cutting the baseboard with a saw. If the surface is solid, then a rough shape of the intended water feature will suffice. The picture below left shows the 'dropped' river bed. If an open framed baseboard is used, 'under sling' the bed. In both cases a base/bed will be needed. To create this, glue and screw – with the aid of spacing blocks – a piece of thin sheet material. This can be of plywood, hardboard, chipboard (particle board) or MDF (medium density fibre board). The base/bed can be set to any depth from 3mm (⅛in) to 25mm (1in) below the 'ground level', which allows for the inclusion of banks, small waterfalls and the like. Having screwed and glued the level base/bed in place, then the banks can be added (if your scale allows).

Polyurethane Foam Board

In recent years dense polyurethane foam has been introduced into the construction industry. This material is strong and its compaction strength makes it very suitable for creating landscapes. It can be cut, sanded, sculptured and painted (with water-based paints only) without any difficulty. There are no problems with white 'beads' as there are with polystyrene when it is cut. The finish can be either left rough or sanded to a smooth surface. Colours range from pink through to blue. Thicknesses of the boards are: 15mm (⅝in), 25mm(1in), 50mm (2in), 75mm (3in), 100mm (4in), 125mm (5in) and 150mm (6in). The sizes of the

A good, level platform onto which the river, lake or pond will be built is most important. Getting this right at the start will pay dividends as you progress.

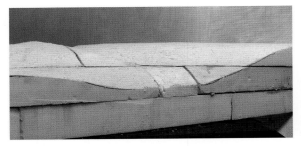

Polyurethane board not only is strong in its compaction strength, but will allow you to sand and cut it without too many issues. Glue layers together using a solvent-free adhesive.

sheets are 1,200×600mm (4×2ft) and 2,400×1,200mm (8×4ft).

RIVER/POND BANKS

These can be made from either a solid material such as MDF, foam board (this is a sandwich of thin, good quality card and a low-density styrene) or cardboard. Set this material at an angle if a river or pond is being modelled, or rather more vertically if a canal is being portrayed. The joint between the bank and the base is then filled with a bead of glue or a thick mix of pre-coloured decorative plaster (The mixing of this is covered in Chapter 1).

Using Polyurethane Board

A river, pond or lake can be formed by sanding a hollow in the board with a sanding block or an electric belt sander. If you intend to have a small change in the levels of the river bed, then now is the time to put this in. A 'rebate' (ledge) can be sanded into the sides to allow for the 'water' to be inserted. Make sure that the rebate is parallel all round.

RIVER/POND BED

Paint lightly thinned PVA glue over the whole structure before adding a thick coat of the plaster mix. This is buttered over the whole area and, where it reaches the pond edges or river banks, a muddy-looking bed is created. To make this feature even more convincing, 'quick dry' it with a hairdryer set at a hot temperature. As PVA has been added to the mix this will make the surface craze and crack a little, giving a convincing look when the model is finished.

The river banks or canal sides can be formed by carefully setting foam board (as in this case) on a bed of glue. The top edges must always be level and parallel.

RIGHT & BELOW: *Sand out a hollow in the foam board to a rough shape of the river bed using a sanding block or an electric belt sander.*

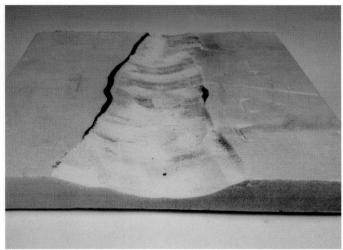

If you want a change in the levels of the water, sand in a rebate to accommodate the plastic sheet that will represent the water. Make sure the rebate sides are parallel.

A small change in levels gives an attractive feature on any model landscape.

A touch of PVA in the plaster mix will aid the bonding. This will craze when a hairdryer is used to fast-dry the surface, but the drying mix will remain adhered to the surface, giving a muddy-looking finish.

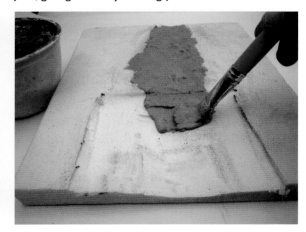

UNDERWATER DETAIL

When all this is dry, the detail can be added. Rocks and boulders make interesting features, and can be modelled from air-drying modelling clay or from lumps of the dried plaster mix. If you are using the air-drying clay, then break off a small piece and roll it around between your thumb and forefinger to form an elongated ball. When this is dry, break it into smaller pieces.

The rocks are then clustered together, glued down with a spot of PVA and set just below the surface of the water on the river/pond bed. Any rocks that need to be showing above the waterline can be added later. These rocks can now be painted with water colours.

Making Underwater Plants

Plants that may be growing in the bed can also be added at this time. Several different materials are suitable.

Clumping foam is a cellulose foam product that has not been broken down into crumbs. It is pulled apart to make a flat, irregular-shaped plant; this is then stuck to the bed with PVA or UHU.

Floor scourers are made from a spun abrasive acrylic material (pot scourers will do but are not so effective). Use the black-coloured type, as these are the coarsest. Cut off a small square and pull it apart until you have a bunch of long, crinkly strands. Spray this with an adhesive and then sprinkle on a pinch of fine latex crumb. Stick this down onto the river/pond bed.

Postiche (doll's hair) is a very versatile product that comes in small shanks. It is good at disappearing behind any crumb that is added to it. The treatment is similar to the scourer except that in this case the material is finer, and you will need less of it to give the same effect.

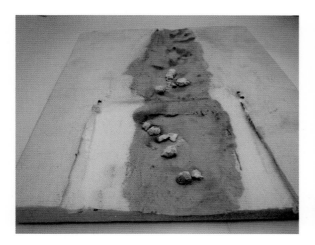

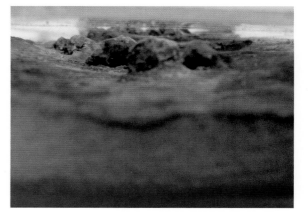

*ABOVE LEFT & RIGHT: **Rocks made from air-drying modelling clay are strategically placed.***

*RIGHT: **Make sure that the tops of the rocks are below the surface of the water.***

Once everything is in place, paint the surface with water-colour paint.

Begin by pinching about 25mm (1in) off the end of the shank, and teasing it out until you have a light, airy ball. Spray this with hair spray and sprinkle on some latex or cellulose crumb before fixing it to the bed with a touch of UHU.

CREATING THE WATER

The water itself can be represented in various ways, but for simplicity I will describe a method that works very well yet is one of the easiest to make.

ACRYLIC PLASTIC SHEET

This is a clear plastic sheet similar to Perspex, but less expensive and available from most DIY superstores. I would recommend the use of one that is 3mm (⅛in) in thickness. There are two types: one for internal glazing and an external-quality one that is designed for greenhouses and the like – the latter is marginally more expensive.

The sheet is used 'in the square': in other words, it is not necessary to cut out the shape of the water feature. Make sure that the sheet is big enough to cover the already-constructed river/pond bed, allowing about 25mm (1in) overhang of the banks. Lay the sheet onto the model and mark the extremities of the banks with a felt-tipped pen, taking into account where any marginal plants may need to be planted.

Mark a line on the sheet to indicate the position of where any submerged rocks or structures might be, and where there is a detail such a drop in the river bed. Now remove the sheet from the model and cut the sheet across this line so that it will sit in the already-formed rebate. Now you can start to detail the 'water.'

PAINTING THE DETAIL

The first step is to coat the underside with an acrylic varnish; this can be either satin or matt; by using acrylic varnishes less time is wasted waiting for each coat to dry. Any painted detail such as algae and water-borne plants can be added quickly and very easily as the matt or satin varnish will take paint more readily than a gloss will.

These details are all painted on the underside with acrylic or water-colour paints. Having ascertained where there is likely to be some algae or pondweed, load the paint brush with paint and a little water; the paint colour will be a light green and needs to be quite thick. Proceed to paint in stripes, much like a well-manicured lawn. Make sure that the 'flow' of the water is observed: in other words, do not paint across the sheet, but down it. If you are representing algae, then this will tend to be in the quiet corners of a pond or stream.

PREPARING ACRYLIC PLASTIC SHEET TO REPRESENT WATER

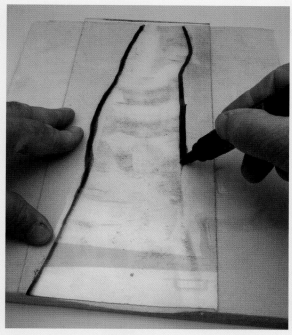

1. A plastic sheet is laid over the bed of the water feature 'in the square', allowing enough overhang.

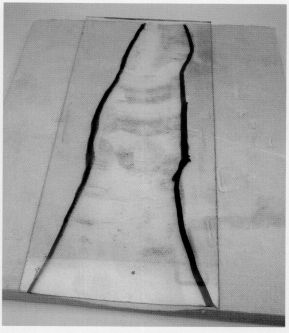

2. Using a felt-tipped pen, mark the edges of the bank and any extra features such as a drop in the river bed.

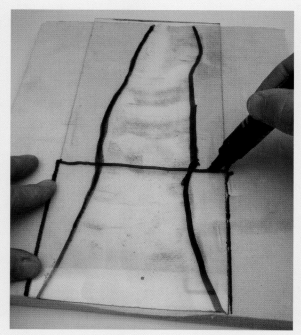

3. This particular detail will involve cutting the sheet across the width: the bottom piece will be bedded in the pre-formed rebate.

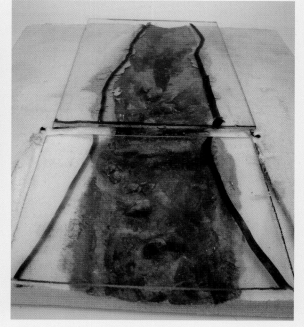

4. Set the sheets temporarily in place to make sure everything is correct.

Turn the plastic sheet over and give the underside one coat of varnish. This can be a matt or satin finish – it's not important to the final finish. Detail is easier to paint onto a matt surface.

Paint on algae and similar-coloured waterborne plants using a heavily loaded brush that is not too wet.

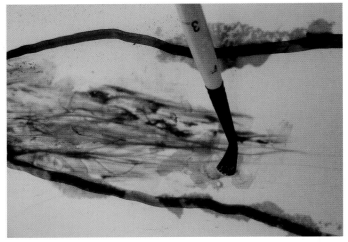

This is replicated by gently stippling the acrylic sheet with a very dry paint-loaded brush.

Another coat of varnish is added, and when that is dry more detail is added in the same manner. It is beneficial to stagger the detail slightly, or at least to set it out of register from the detail above. This will, after several coats, start to give an effect of depth. It is a very quick and easy method of detailing, for the varnishes will dry very quickly in a warm atmosphere.

MEDIUM- TO FAST-FLOWING WATER

Flowing water will drag most waterborne plants with its flow. If replicating medium- to fast-flowing water,

add pre-coloured fibres or strands of sisal string, plumber's hemp (now quite rare) or a proprietary product such as 'Field Grass' from Woodland Scenics. The latter is probably the best I have found. It is supplied in various shades (a different shade in each pack) and is approximately 60mm (2½in) in length, with very straight strands.

Lay some strands of 'Field Grass' carefully into wet varnish that has been painted on the underside of the sheet. Bend the strands to replicate the way that flowing water bends waterborne plants.

Alternatively, to add even further depth, attach postiche (treated in way described earlier) to the

A medium- to fast-flowing stream or river will take any vegetation with it, so when representing this make sure all detail 'goes with the flow'.

Woodland Scenics 'Field Grass' is ideal for representing underwater plants.

underside of the sheet with a touch of clear glue. This kind of underwater foliage would normally be in the quieter stretches of the water: in a pond close to the edge underneath an overhanging tree, for instance, or around the edge of an island.

RIPPLES

Turn the plastic sheet over and suspend it on a couple of blocks of wood. To begin, add a much thicker coat of acrylic matt or satin varnish. This is then stippled lightly to represent the ripples. Play the warm air from a hairdryer over the wet varnish to speed up the drying process. The warm air should be played along

the surface rather than directly down onto it: the thick coat of varnish will be pushed up further by the warm air, retaining these preformed ripples.

An alternative method that can be used to create this movement involves the use of PVA glue, and gives a really good representation of the wind blowing across the water. Gently paint PVA into patterns of ripples with a small artist's brush, and carefully dry it with a hairdryer on a warm setting rather than a very hot one. Applying this method where there are rocks will greatly enhance the overall impression of water being forced to go round an obstacle. Lightly and carefully stipple the PVA glue around them.

MODELLING WATERBORNE PLANTS

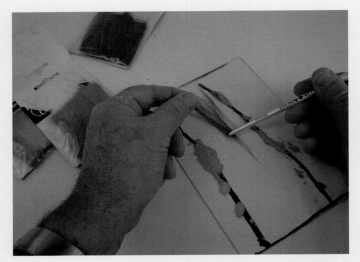

1. Carefully paint on a coat of varnish before sorting out a few strands of Field Grass and placing them into the wet coating, making sure that you 'go with the flow'.

2. Finally, apply another layer of the matt varnish. Keep on doing this until you have attained the desired effect.

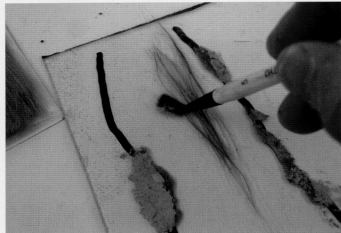

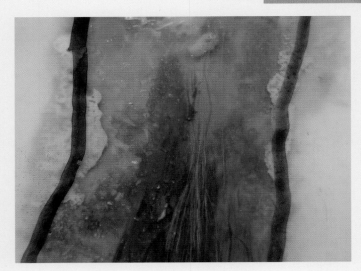

3. It looks a little untidy, but when the plastic sheet is turned over the effect is quite worth the effort.

Note how the waterborne plants 'flow' towards the break to a lower level in the river bed. These plants can be represented with field grass laid carefully in wet varnish.

Beneath the surface, detail such as this is always worth the effort.

A light breeze creates a few ripples here and there, but not over the whole surface – a good point to remember when modelling large areas of fresh water.

The effect created here was achieved with the aid of a hairdryer. By blowing warm air over the surface of a thick coat of acrylic varnish, ripples were formed. This is a scene in the scale of 4mm/ft on John Sinfield's superb 'Snow Drop Railway'.

A third way of creating ripples is to use Heavy Structure Gel. This is an acrylic gel that can be used to create larger ripples, such as tumbling or 'confused' water, the wash from a boat, or the smaller wash from ducks and swans.

This gel, when applied fairly heavily, will not 'slump'. Wherever it is put, it stays, rather than spreading out like a varnish would. It starts off a milky white colour when it is first applied, making it easy to see how it is going to look when it dries; when it has cured the finish is semi-clear.

Heavy Structure Gel also lends itself to forming rough water, such as the bottom of a waterfall, weirs and rapids, all of which have 'confused or angry' water.

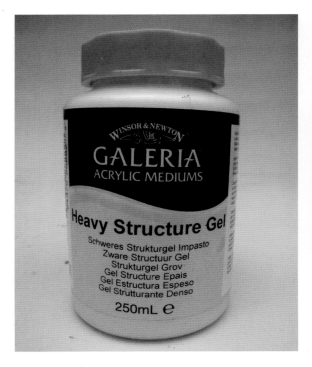

ABOVE: The beauty of Heavy Structure Gel is that it will not 'slump' – it will stay where it is put instead of spreading out as a varnish might do.

LEFT: Heavy Structure Gel is ideal for creating larger ripples, tumbling and 'confused or angry' water.

Paint on the gel with a No. 3 paint brush, move it into position and leave it to dry. As this is an acrylic medium and water-based, washing the brush after use is not difficult – just use warm, soapy water. Paint over the whole surface with a high gloss acrylic paint or an oil-based varnish.

ADDING PLANTS

Surface-borne water plants such as water lilies or broad-leafed pond weed can either be painted on or cut out of paper and stuck on. Where the smaller scales are concerned, cutting out the lily pads might prove problematical, so they are best painted on. It is far better to add these after all the paintwork is dry.

Marginal plants such as bulrush, iris or reeds can be glued on after the top coat of varnish has dried; the making of these plants is covered in Chapter 3. As they are fairly tall plants, they must be supported in some way. This can be achieved by drilling holes in the acrylic sheet in readiness for planting. A group of these holes will allow quite a realistic planting of the reeds.

These are pushed though the sheet and down to the bed of the feature. The finish of the water is clear so it might be possible to see right down to the mud. It is not necessary to push all of the reeds to the full depth just the outer ones in the group – I always think this is a nice touch.

The lily pads here have been both cut out of pre-coloured paper and painted onto the water.

1. Drill a few holes at the water's edge in readiness to take the plants.

2. Add a touch of glue to the base and pass the plant plug through the hole.

3. Very soon an attractive group of 'water's edge' planting appears.

COMPLETING THE 'WATER'

Lay the sheet over the bed, fixing it down with a bead of hot-melt glue. The landscape can now be continued down to the water's edge. Paint a coat of PVA over the surrounding area to act as a bonding agent. Butter the plaster mix over the edge of the plastic sheet and up to the line previously drawn with the felt-tipped pen. Feather the edge with a paint brush and a drop of water so that it all blends together.

CANALS AND CANAL BASINS

DETAILING BELOW THE WATERLINE

A slightly different approach is required in this case. After you have made the base/bed and the walls on either side of the canal, paint decorative plaster up to the top edge of the walls, cleaning off anything above it and making sure the edge is level. Next, lay the plastic sheet on top of the walls, allowing a small overhang on either side, mark the extremities of the water (the straight line of the up stands below, on which the sheet sits), and remove the sheet from the model.

Paint on a coat or two of varnish and add detail as before. Bear in mind that canal water tends to be murky: a dark colour such as a green/brown should be added to the varnish, just to give it some body. As we are using an acrylic varnish, then the paint must also be acrylic. Proceed to paint the underside; when this is dry, the topside can be treated to a coat of varnish. Any ripples that may be required are added, and this is then followed by the top coat of a high-gloss varnish.

The completed sheet is then stuck onto the up stand using hot-melt glue or UHU. Any walls should be glued on top of the plastic sheet, making sure there is a good, tight fit. Vertical mooring timbers can be added before or after the walls are fixed; where water laps around these piles, a small ripple can be introduced. These ripples are made using the methods described earlier, with either Heavy Structure Gel or PVA. Be careful not to put too much on around the posts – remember that too little is far preferable to too much.

OTHER METHODS OF MODELLING WATER

Casting resin is used quite a lot in our hobby, but is a rather messy way of creating water and leaves too many openings for disasters.

Another method is to paint on many coats of varnish, which is a little better than resin though it will take a fair while to build up a respectable depth. There is the danger that the varnish will stay soft and 'squidgy'. Added to this is the threat of the dreaded meniscus – this is a curve (concave or convex) in a surface that is formed when two meeting surfaces have differing molecular structures. A meniscus is evident when the varnish curves (concave) up the wall of a canal. Reeds previously planted at the waterside will also draw the varnish up by capillary attraction, forming an unsightly curve. The final danger that you will encounter using these methods is shrinkage, which occurs when one or the other of the surfaces dries out. A crack will appear down one or both edges, which will prove difficult to disguise.

WATERFALLS

How do we represent a vast amount of moving water that is supposedly falling from a great height? This is plainly not an easy subject to model convincingly, but there are a couple of methods that will give a good representation of falling water.

THE HOT-MELT GLUE METHOD

Hot-melt glue guns are used for a variety of tasks in industry, and by hobbyists worldwide. They come in many guises and prices, but they all do one thing: melt sticks of glue by passing the stick through a heated element and then out through a nozzle.

How glue guns work depends on the price and make – some, for example, allow you to vary the temperature – but the recommendation here is to purchase one that is fairly cheap, will take glue sticks that have an average diameter of 10mm (⅜in) and has a trigger mechanism; this will force the glue stick past the heat source without too of much of a problem. The cheapest tool requires thumb pressure.

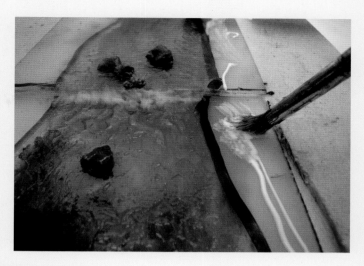

1. Glue the plastic sheet into place. Coat the surrounding area with PVA.

2. Butter on the pre-coloured plaster mix.

3. Feather the edges with a paint brush dipped in water. Leave to dry before moving to the next stage.

continued overleaf

4. *The mix is very dark here but it will dry to a lighter colour. Note the top left and bottom right.*

5. *Planting here took place after the ground had been brought down to the water's edge.*

6. *The depth of the water is highlighted by the addition of underwater plants.*

There is nothing quite like a photograph to give inspiration and guidance when modelling a difficult subject such as cascading water.

First of all make sure that the rear of the waterfall i.e. the rock face or the river bed where there is a distinct drop in the levels, is painted in a dark colour. This gives the effect of wet rock and adds some depth. The hot-melt glue gun now comes into play but only after it has become very very hot. Bear in mind the average glue gun is not that sophisticated. It will take around about five minutes to attain the optimum temperature.

Starting at the top of the cliff or rock face, allow the glue to drizzle down the water course, keeping the gun about 50mm (2in) away. Strings of glue will fall on to the water course. This method has to be very controlled for two reasons. First, if the build-up of hot glue is too fast, then all of the applied glue will end up at the end of the waterfall in an almighty pile of unwanted glue that doesn't much resemble falling water! Second, be very careful where the glue is applied for being careful at this stage will reduce the spread of glue across the face of the work. Taking care with the application here is time well spent. Drag the hot nozzle through the cooling glue and pull it down the face of the work to give it a cascading effect. Once this has cooled, highlights can be added as described under 'The Dry Brush Method' on p.88.

THE SILICONE SEALANT METHOD

Take a sheet of clear plastic or glass approximately 75mm (3in) longer than the height of the waterfall or length of the rapids and lay it flat on a workbench. Take a fresh tube of translucent building silicone sealant and, with a skeleton gun, squeeze several thin beads of the silicone sealant down the length of the sheet, keep the beads very close together. Next, drag a piece of spare plastic or a palette knife down the length of the beads of silicone, making sure to take the plastic square off and over the edge of the sheet. Do this a couple of times with the lightest of touches.

Set this aside to cure by leaving it in a warm environment for some considerable time. Then, with care, peel the sheet of rubbery transparent 'water' from the sheet of plastic or glass. This will then be the waterfall and is hung, for want of a better word, from the top of the rock face. Cut the sheet of 'angry water' to size with a pair of sharp scissors – using a sharp knife is more difficult.

1. A skeleton gun, silicone building mastic and a plastic spreader are all essential items when waterfalls and 'angry or confused water' is being modelled with silicone sealant.

2. A sheet of glass or plastic is also essential.

3. Several beads of the transparent silicone are laid close to each other.

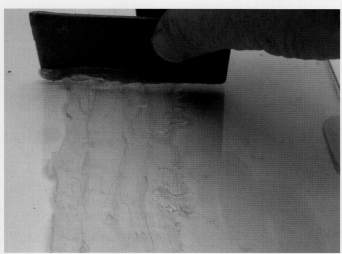

4. Take the plastic spreader and drag it along the length of the silicone. Do this several times with the lightest of touches.

5. The silicone will take a while to cure, so leave it in a warm room until it has become a rubbery sheet.

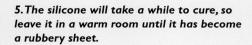

continued overleaf

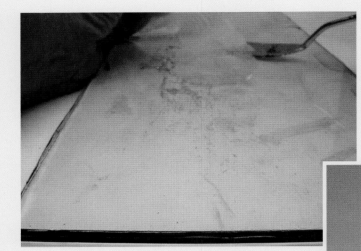

6. Carefully prise the cured silicone sheet away from the backing (glass or plastic sheet).

7. Now we have the makings of cascading or angry water.

8. Cut the rubbery sheet to size and shape with a pair of sharp scissors.

9. Tack the top section with a small bead of silicone and let it cure.

10. Do the same at the bottom, this time with a little more silicone, and rough it up to represent angry water.

Attach the trimmed 'water' to the top of the water course with several small beads of silicone sealant. Let it drop down the cliff or rocky face, attach the end to the model and leave to cure.

DISGUISING THE TOP JOIN

Where the top meets up with an already-formed river, the cured sealant can be carefully blended. Bed the joint between the two surfaces by using a wooden spatula (coffee stirrer) or palette knife loaded with some silicone sealant.

At the bottom where the 'water' connects with the riverbed, lightly stipple the curing silicone sealant. Here, the rough water can be enhanced further by stippling Heavy Structure Gel onto the cooled hot-melt glue or cured silicone and the previously prepared river bed.

All this is then carefully coloured and dry brushed.

THE DRY BRUSH METHOD

Load a No.7 paint brush with white acrylic paint and then wipe off most of the paint, leaving the brush almost dry. Next, flick or quickly drag this across the high points of the cascading 'water', leaving just a trace of paint behind. The same method is used at the base of the waterfall, where the water is now so aerated that white foam is very evident.

Finish with a high-gloss acrylic medium this time rather than an oil-based varnish. When viewed in certain light conditions the water will 'sparkle'.

WEIRS AND RAPIDS

The movement of water is difficult to represent. Small changes in the riverbed level or a narrowing of the banks will cause rapids and small waterfalls. Modelling these will add greatly to the realism.

As the water drops down the rock face the spray makes the surrounding rock glisten. This can be represented by painting the rock face with a high-gloss acrylic medium.

Tumbling, angry water that is being squeezed between the rocks gives a great deal of information for the modeller.

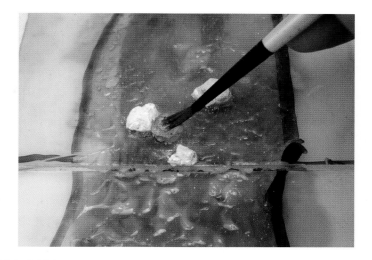

Glue the rocks to the river surface and add a touch of colour to them before proceeding with the angry water.

Apply Heavy Structure Gel around the rocks.

Be careful to follow the flow of the water.

Taking rapids first, begin by laying the river bed. Set the surface (plastic sheet) and add boulders and stones, which can be made from air-drying modelling clay. Press and glue these to the water's surface after flattening the bottom edge. If there are any rocks below the surface and you want make them appear above it, now is the time to glue these on. Make the shapes similar to those that are beneath. Set them directly above the submerged rocks and add a touch of colour to the rocks before applying the angry 'water'. Load a No.2 brush with some Heavy Structure Gel and paint this around the stones, being careful to show the flow. This gel is very good for portraying small waves and ripples, and any brush strokes that you may leave in will remain if they are not smoothed out. This will give a very good interpretation of angry water.

Work the gel around the stones and in some cases up and over the top where, with a flick of the brush,

A shallow drop in the levels of the river bed can be shown by using Heavy Structure Gel.

Paint it on and drag it over the edge as water would flow in reality, and let it dry.

the gel will remain suspended and dry. Once all this has dried and set, the dry brushing technique is employed. Pass the brush over the top of the waves and coat it all with a high-gloss medium.

Where there is a sharp drop in the water level, then a weir-like appearance can be modelled. This is achieved by the judicious use of hot-melt glue or a silicone sealant. Hot-melt glue is applied with the flow of the river and, using the hot nozzle, stroke the glue as it cools. Apply the dry bushing technique to highlight the fast-flowing water.

With silicone sealant the same process is applied, but this time drag a small spatula through the sealant, working very rapidly before it starts to set, leaving the resulting 'bunching' at the base to set. Build this up to give a good representation of frothing turbulent water and dry brush to highlight the fast water.

Here there is a bigger drop in the water level.

Hot-melt glue or transparent silicone mastic can be used.

CHAPTER FIVE

TREES

Trees are large: so large that trees made in a true scale will overpower and dwarf our railways and dioramas. Unless we are modelling a specific scene that has a tree as its only centrepiece, some compression – often a great deal of compression – will be needed. However, a tree is a majestic thing of beauty, and our intention must be to reflect this fantastic majesty. Observation is the key.

THE OBSERVATION AND SIZING OF A TREE

To 'size up' a tree to model, as rule of thumb take the height of an average semi-detached house and multiply it 2–2¼ times. Put another way, the length of a mainline coach turned on its end. This is the average height in model form of a mature tree, compressed just enough for it to look right. Even the common silver birch will rise to become a magnificent specimen.

A walk down any tree-lined street will give you an idea of what I mean.

The 'spread' – the umbrella effect of the branches – has to be in relation to the thickness of the trunk. Many models have too spindly a trunk topped by a massive canopy. This rarely happens in reality as either the trunk will snap or the tree will topple. The root spread of, for instance, a weeping willow is the mirror image of the canopy of leaves above.

When you make a tree for the first time, choose something not too ambitious: a relatively common tree such as a hawthorn or an apple tree would be a good starting point. If possible, take photographs of it in its naked winter form and when fully clothed in summer. It is a good idea to have a tree recognition book with a good selection of photographs and silhouette drawings to hand. These will give you a good feel, but nothing beats actually going and looking at a real live specimen.

This is classic parkland of the Georgian period in the British Isles. It shows the great size to which trees can grow when they are allowed to mature. Their crowns are noticeable in this early spring photograph.

The spread is an important part of the model as much as the height. Stand with your back pressed up against the trunk of the tree and look straight up to obtain a proper sense of the width of the canopy. A similar thing should be done with your models but, as you can't stand with your back to the trunk, turn your model over. Look at the underside and if you can see an umbrella effect with the canopy fairly evenly spread, then you have got things about right.

As mentioned in the introduction to this book there are trees that will grow almost anywhere and there are those that are very regional in their distribution, so be very careful when setting out to model a tree. Get the right specimen in the area you are modelling and the realism will abound.

When studying old photographs of railways you will see that the embankments were devoid of trees. The lengthsman – whose responsibility it was to keep the track and embankments in a good and safe condition – would keep it that way. It was done to keep fire risk to a minimum, but is less important in the post-steam era and we find most cuttings and embankments are now covered with trees. When modelling a line up to the end of the steam, do not put in too many large trees on an embankment, but if a modern line is being modelled, even in an urban scene there will be these 'weeds'.

THE PROCESS BEGINS

There are tree kits on the market: pewter (sometimes known as white metal), cast resin and plastic armatures with foliage material thrown in to complete the kit. Whilst good, they are mostly very repetitive in their shape and will lend themselves better to middle distance grouping. For a better result, making your tree from scratch is best.

Looking up the trunk of a beech. The strength in those limbs is fantastic! Imagine the weight when in full summer attire.

Turn the model over and look at the canopy from the underside. If the canopy looks fairly well spread then you have done it about right.

Painter's caulk, plated florist's wire and florist's tape.

When modelling trees various materials can be used. These include florist's wire, painter's caulk, copper wire, hot-melt glue, panel adhesive and of course decorative plaster (Artex).

FLORIST'S WIRE

Florist's wire is either plastic-coated (often green) or just plain plated mild steel and is sold in small straight bundles. Start by working up from the bottom of a bundle, twisting strands together and binding with florist's tape (which can be can be either green or brown) along with the intersections. As progress is made up the tree, the main limbs and trunk are made in the same way. Make sure you have covered everything with the tape.

Now run your fingers over the tape, smoothing the edges as you go. When you are happy with the result apply a coat or two of either 'Flexi-Bark' or Sandtex paint. Flexi-Bark is a precoloured flexible paint supplied by Green Scene. Sandtex is an exterior masonry paint, which is also flexible when dry. Both have small 'bits' in the paint, although Sandtex does come in a 'smooth' finish. The paint can be quite aggressive, as the name 'Sandtex' implies – sand is one of the ingredients. This will wear the brush bristles away fairly quickly.

If a thicker trunk is required, then an application of painter's caulk is necessary. Apply this by using a mastic gun (also known as a skeleton gun) as detailed below.

MODELLING TREES WITH FLORIST'S WIRE

A closer look at florist's tape. This tape is used by florists to bind flower stems together; we use it in a similar way to bind our branches and trunks together.

MIDDLE & BOTTOM: Twist the wires together, working up the tree, and bind this with the florist's tape, including all the intersecting branches. When this is complete, smooth the tape between your fingers.

PAINTER'S CAULK

Painter's caulk is very good for adding bulk to a tree (see box overleaf). It is sometimes mistaken for silicone sealant but is far from that. It is an acrylic gap filler designed to take paint and is water-soluble, so it can be worked with a paint brush whilst still wet. It will dry to a rubbery finish. It is manufactured in several colours from white through to brown and comes in a tube.

Cut a small amount off the end of the nozzle leaving a hole about 6mm (¼in) diameter. Gently squeeze the trigger on the skeleton gun so that a small amount of filler appears out of the tube's nozzle, then carefully spread it around the trunk and main branches of the tree. Finish it off with a paint brush and a touch of water, blending in around the intersection of the branches.

Have a piece of card or glass handy and squeeze a bead onto it. This will act as a palette, allowing you to dip your paint brush or palette knife into it should you need to add small detail to your tree. This is a simple process and a very effective one.

When your work has cured the caulk will allow small amounts of adjustment to be made to the shape of the tree. The tree can then be painted with acrylic paints that have been thinned down a little.

COPPER WIRE METHODS

Copper wire is obtainable from all manner of sources but perhaps the best supply is from the larger DIY superstores or electrical wholesalers. The most common and probably the best are 13amp ring main wire, earth bonding wire and lighting flex. If you can get industrial and/or panel wire (tri-rated) cable, this is also very useful.

FINE MULTI-STRAND WIRE
2mm Scale and Bigger
This method gives a very detailed finish but requires lots of time and patience. You will need multi-stranded fine wire such as that found in 'panel wire' (tri-rated is the technical term). Lighting flex is also useful, but you will need quite a lot of it if you are making a fairly large tree.

Start by stripping back the outer sheathing to expose the fine wires; put a few short lengths aside from the main bundle, which will be used to bind the branches together. Work down from the top, twisting off just a few strands. These form the uppermost branches which, in most cases, are small and require only a few twists: because the wires are very fine a more 'twiggy look' is achieved. Work down and round the main bundle, taking off bigger numbers of wires to form the branches. These are bound together with the few strands set aside earlier.

The further down the trunk, the more regular the binding. Give all the branches a touch of solder to stop them from untwisting. If the original bundle is not long enough, intertwine more wires to create an extended trunk or branch. Again, a touch of solder will help with the rigidity.

On finally reaching the roots, leave a few strands to twist together; these will form a tap root which, in real life, anchors the tree to the ground. On the model this will enable you fix the tree to the landscape. Spreading surface roots can also be twisted off at this time. These stabilize the tree and help brace it against the weather, and in model form they will add to the realism. Again, all bindings and twists should be touch-soldered to give strength and rigidity. A fine multi-cored solder is useful for this particular job, used with a 25-watt or larger soldering iron.

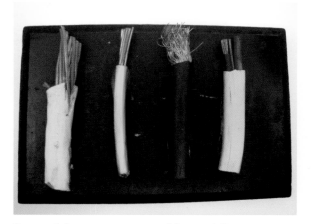

Some of the copper wire used for modelling trees. From the left: Heavy 3-phase wire, 8mm earth wire, panel wire (tri-rated), 30 amp domestic cable.

USING PAINTER'S CAULK TO BULK UP A TREE

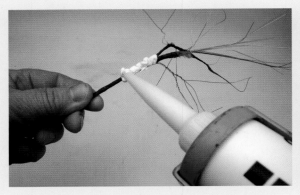

1. Bulk up the tree with the painter's caulk carefully applied.

2. The caulk is now ready to be moved about, which is easy to do while it is still wet.

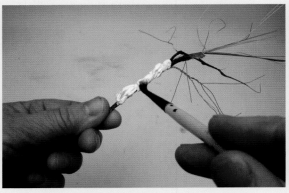

3. A paint brush loaded with water can move the caulk up and around the tree. Include the main branches but not the single strands: these can be painted with paint or 'Flexi Bark'.

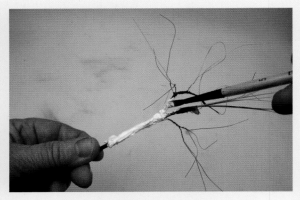

4. Blend the caulk into the intersecting branches.

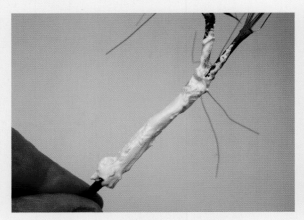

5. The trunk is now ready for some further texturing.

6. With a dry brush, drag the bristles through the caulk to form the fissures in the bark.

The whole tree is then checked for balance (the spread of the branches) and then washed under a hot tap to remove all residues of flux.

Multi-Gauge Wire Trees

This is my favoured method of tree construction: it is simple, quick and produces a tree that is very adaptable. Summer or winter trees can easily be made, with as many branches as needed added, or left out, during the construction.

4mm Scale Trees and Bigger

The skeleton or armature is the basis for all that follows, for it is this that will eventually give you a realistic tree. I liken it to constructing a building; if the foundations are correct then all that follows will also be correct.

To make the armature, strip away the outer sheathing, leaving about 60mm (2⅛in) on the end; this is useful when soldering the branches as it will give you something to hold that is insulated from the hot copper wire. If, however, you are making a particularly intricate tree, discard the sheathing altogether.

Using 8mm earthing cable (this cable is sheathed with green and yellow PVC), twist a couple of strands, push them into a piece of brass tube and then solder them together. The brass tube will act as a plug and eventually becomes the tap root.

Cut off 150mm (6in) of scrap brass tube. This tube should have an internal diameter that will match the outside diameter of the tap 'root plug'. Grip this long piece of tube vertically in a vice and plug the skeleton/armature tree into the resulting 'socket'. This will allow the skeleton/armature to be turned whilst work on an individual branch is carried out.

Twist up the trunk and then any main branches that may be required. Any extra branches that you may need can be added to the skeleton at this stage. It is useful to have a hot soldering iron close by and, as you work your way up the tree, touch-solder all twisted-off branches. If any branches are too long, bend them back on themselves until the end reaches the original intersection; twist these together and form a loop, and touch-solder the loop at the intersection. The top of the loop is snipped with a pair of wire cutters and straightened; this will give you two branches from the one piece of wire.

*LEFT & ABOVE: **These models were all made using the wire skeleton/armature as a starting block.***

Push a few twists of wire into a short piece of brass tube and solder them together; this becomes a 'plug'.

The outside diameter of the 'plug' matches the inside diameter of the scrap brass tube that becomes the 'socket'.

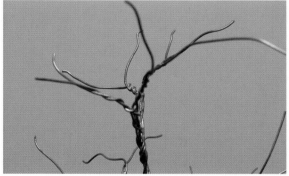

ABOVE: The end of the 'socket' is held in a vice and the tree armature is placed in it. This will allow the tree to be turned as work progresses.

ABOVE RIGHT: The skeleton is twisted up along with the main branches.

RIGHT: This example shows how a simple tree can be formed.

OPPOSITE MAIN PICTURE & INSET: It is a good idea if you can get a photo or two of your chosen tree, preferably through the seasons. The first photograph of this very old ash was taken into the sun to highlight its shape.

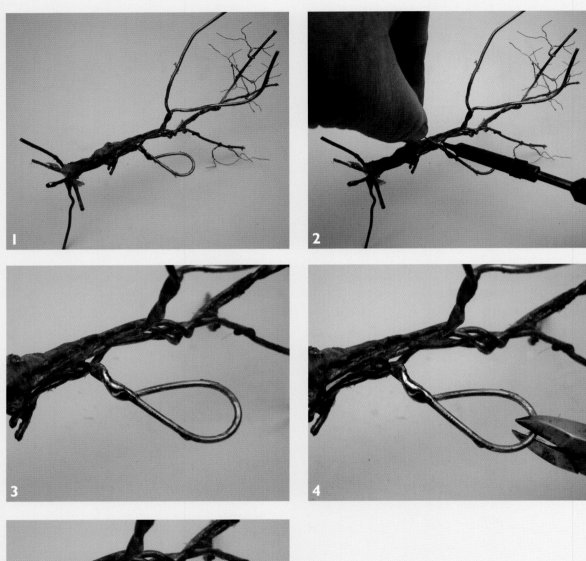

Any long branches that look out of place can be looped back on themselves, twisted together at the intersection of the trunk and touched with solder. The top of the loop is snipped and the cut opened out into two branches. This gives two branches from one.

THE FINER BRANCHES ('TWIGGERY')

Once the skeleton/armature has been completed you can turn your attention to the finer detail such as the twigs. It depends on the time of year your model is set as to whether the tree is a heavily clothed (fully foliated) summer tree or a bare winter tree; in the latter case a lot more detail is necessary as you will see all of the branches and twiggy bits.

To make the 'twiggery', take finer wires such as those found in lighting flex and cut them to a length of about 50mm (2in). Fold one or two strands in half around a small jeweller's screwdriver shaft; the shaft should be the approximate diameter of the copper wire skeleton branch. Twist the wires in a similar manner to the skeleton; you will then have several 'Y' shapes. Remove the screwdriver from the wire leaving a loop, and slide the loop over the main branch of the tree.

Most of these little branches should be grouped in odd numbers. They will hang down like bats hanging on the branch of a tree. Space these twigs along the branch, but not too evenly. Touch the loops with a suitable flux, then with the hot soldering iron and solder wire. The solder will adhere the loop to the main branch and run down all the twists of the twigs, making them rigid.

This tree has less 'twiggery' as it will have a full coat of leaves.

'Twiggery' can be very noticeable on a winter tree but may not be necessary on a summer tree, which will usually be 'fully clothed'.

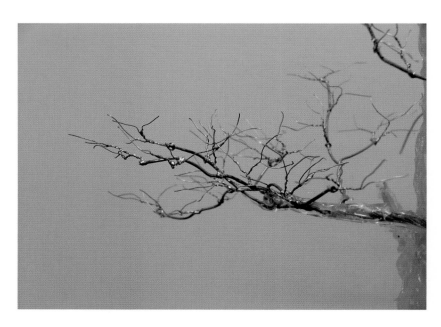

MODELLING A BARE TREE

1. Fine wire from lighting flex or panel wire (tri-rated) is ideal for the smaller branches or twigs.

2. Take a couple of lengths of wire and fold them in half.

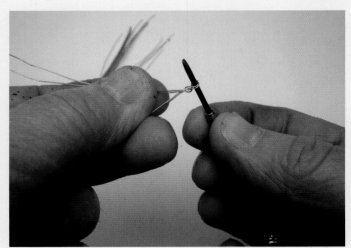

3. Twist them around a small screwdriver.

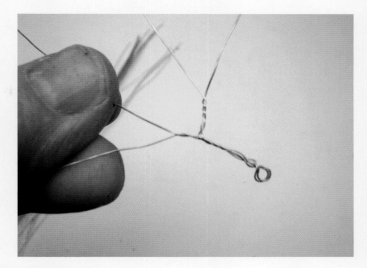

4. This will give you a loop that allows you to pass the twigs over the main branch. Continue to twist up the wire and form further shorter twigs.

5. If a twig is too long, fold it back on itself and twist the end and intersection together. This should give you a loop.

6. Slide the twigs over the branch and group them in odd numbers if you can. Dab on some flux and touch-solder the loops to the branch.

continued overleaf

7. Let the 'twiggery' hang down like bats hanging from a tree.

8. Grip the end of the branch with a pair of pliers and twist it around, making the twigs look more natural.

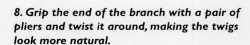

9. Touch-solder the loops.

10. Two 'twigs' from one wire loop.

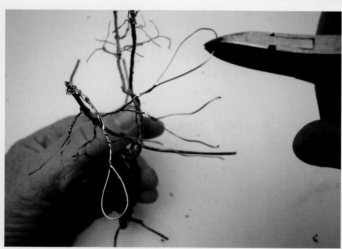

11. Cut the loop with a pair of snips.

12. Straighten the curve out.

continued overleaf

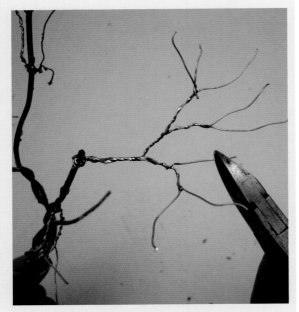

13. You can now trim back any twigs that are a little too long.

Take hold of the end of the main branch with a pair of pliers and twist the branch so that the 'twiggery' then becomes either horizontal or vertical, depending on the kind of tree being modelled. When you are happy with the overall appearance, wash the tree with hot water.

THICKENING THE TRUNK USING A HOT-MELT GLUE GUN

Thicken up the main branches and trunk using a hot-melt glue gun, leaving the finer branches alone as applying the hot-melt glue to these will prove to be a very tricky and difficult operation. Be careful not to put too much on at any one time, or the glue will creep down the trunk and end up in a large pool around the root area. As the glue starts cooling, the shape of the trunk and main branches can be aided by rolling the tree between thumb and forefinger. Tip the tree up and down so that the glue settles to a reasonable shape. After the hot-melt glue has cooled it becomes a semi-transparent milky colour; in this state the outline and proportions of your tree can ascertained.

Note: Be very aware that the copper wire conducts heat very efficiently.

14. Continue round the whole tree in this manner.

It will be very likely that the trunk will have to be made a lot thicker to make it a more realistic-looking tree.

THICKENING THE TRUNK USING A HOT-MELT GLUE GUN

Starting with the trunk, build up the hot-melt glue carefully, letting each application cool a little before applying some more. Work up the tree and along the main branches; don't try to cover the 'twiggery', as this will prove very difficult. Turn the tree round, up and down as the glue cools to allow the glue to run into an acceptable shape. When everything has settled down, the bark can be applied.

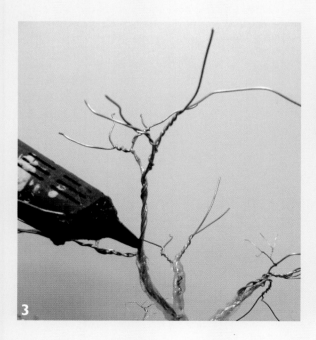

continued overleaf

This is a close study of an ancient Scots pine's bark. It shows the platelet pattern and how deep the fissures are. Not all old trees have the same texture: the bark of the beech shown at the start of this chapter is relatively smooth.

ADDING THE BARK

You are now coming to the interesting part. This next section will make or break the look of your tree.

Proceed by adding a coat of PVA glue to all branches and twigs. This is to aid the bonding of any subsequent coatings such as a pre-coloured decorative plaster mix. For most trees a grey mixture of decorative plaster is used, though there are a few exceptions such as silver birch. Most tree trunks are not an obvious brown colour but tend to be grey and, when wet, almost black.

MIXING THE DECORATIVE PLASTER

Lightly thin the mix and paint it on to the tree using a No. 3 paint brush. Leave that coat to dry. Several more coats can be added, the last of which should be painted on using a slightly stiffer paint brush. The detail of the bark is worked with this the last coat, by lightly dragging the loaded paint brush down through the mix.

An oak's bark will have vertical fissures.

COATING THE TREE WITH DECORATIVE PLASTER

1. Coat the trunk with pre-mixed decorative plaster.

2. Working your way up the tree, cover all of the branches and 'twiggery'.

continued overleaf

3. Make sure you paint these previously uncoated parts with some PVA – this will aid the bonding process.

4. The final finish should look something like this.

The last coat will be given over to texturing the bark.

How you do this depends on the type of tree as to how the bark is represented. A Scots pine, for instance, will have a deep platelet pattern, while for an oak the bark would be represented by vertical strokes. All of this work must be completely dry before moving to the next stage.

COLOURING THE BARK

The colouring of the bark is achieved with the use of water colour paints (*see box overleaf*). Start with a dark colour, loading the brush with plenty of water and then a touch of colour. Allow this to flow into the fissures of the bark: the water will flow quite quickly and disappear into the trunk. Keep on loading the brush, and by following the previous line the colour will begin to build.

The colour/shades can be varied, but do bear in mind which side of the tree is most in the shade. There will probably be some form of moss on the shady side, which is represented by a touch of green paint sparingly applied. With less water on the brush, add a few different shades lightly flicked across the surface, so that fissures in the bark and any other detail will show up. A final fix is achieved by spraying with a matte medium or similar artist's sealer.

WIRE AND SISAL STRING METHOD

There are many layouts that have this type of tree on them, and in bulk they give the impression of a pine or conifer wood. The method for making them is quite old but none the less still has a place in modelling. The process given here was described and taught to me by the late Jack Kine, who was a professional special effects man for the BBC. It works well in the 2mm and 4mm scales, but not so well in 7mm scale and bigger.

For 4mm scale, start by taking a piece of wire about 400mm (16in) long and bend it into an L shape, making sure the limbs of the L are of equal length. Cut some sisal strands to a length of about 50–60mm (2–2½in). Complete your preparations by driving a nail into the workbench and then cutting its head off.

Lay the L-shaped wire flat and run quick-drying glue such as UHU down the length of one limb. Lay the sisal strands onto the glued wire, ensuring they are fairly even. Next, fold the other limb onto the sisal strands, leaving a small gap on the bend so it can form a loop, and let the glue dry. Now, slide the wire loop over the nail; as the nail has had its head cut off, it will be easy to remove the tree later on. Insert the two

COLOURING THE BARK

Float in a dark colour first of all as this will accentuate any deep fissures. Shady parts will have some moss growing, which is represented by sparingly applied green paint. Pick out any detail by lightly flicking the paint brush across the surface.

ends of the wire into a hand drill or wheel brace and then turn for approximately eighteen revolutions, then remove the wire from the drill/brace and slip the loop off the nail.

This then resembles something like a bottle brush and can be formed into a tree by snipping off the loop at the top, cutting the branches into shape and then spraying with black paint. Whilst the paint is wet, dip it and roll into a container of scatter crumb and then a final fixing of acrylic matt varnish.

BALSA TREES

I came across this method when reading some old railroading magazines from America; it is a really good method of replicating tall pines and similar trees. It is always good to batch-build these trees as you will never have enough.

Take a length of squared-up balsa wood the length and general size you need, depending on the scale in which you are modelling. With a knife or a sheet of coarse glass paper, round off the square edges with gentle longitudinal strokes, roughly tapering the length of balsa as you go. It is not really necessary to have a truly round trunk, indeed a uniform trunk would not look right, so any slight imperfections will add to the natural look. Leave a small, squared-off section at the end or bottom of the tree trunk and push a short nail or cocktail stick into the base; this will allow you to hold the tree comfortably either in a pin chuck or vice.

Squared-up balsa wood.

THE BARK

The bark is just a matter of passing a fine wire brush also known as a burnishing brush up and down the length of the trunk to replicate the fissures in the bark. It will depend on the level of detail required as to how much pressure is applied to the brush. If the tree has been subjected to a lightning strike, then a split is required in the bark: this is done by using a scalpel or craft knife to cut a V into the balsa, and then gently passing the wire brush over it so that the grain lifts, leaving a rough finish.

PAINTING THE TRUNK

Water-colours are used to colour the trunk. Start with dark grey or even black to bring up the bark features. Note that the water will swell the balsa after the first application, so let the trunk dry a little before the next step. Follow the first coat with shades of grey or grey/browns; these subsequent coats should be applied with a little less water. Photographs are useful here as a reference to the shape of the tops (canopy) and colour of the bark. There will usually be a large amount of trunk showing if you are modelling lodge pole pines, hemlocks or similar trees. Set aside to dry.

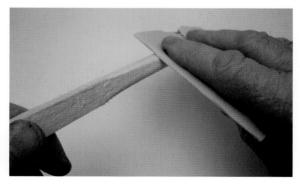

TOP AND ABOVE: *Rub off the edges into an irregular shape and taper the stick to a point.*

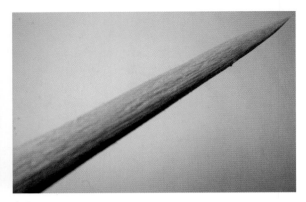

*ABOVE LEFT AND RIGHT: **Roughen the surface to form bark-like fissures.***

Paint the stick with a diluted dark grey or black water-colour and let it thoroughly dry out.

Statice (Caspia) is ideal for making tall pines.

NATURAL MATERIALS FOR THE BRANCHES/FOLIAGE

While the trunk is drying you can start sorting out your branches. How you make them will depend on the type of tree you are modelling. A good all-rounder is a dried plant/grass called Statice in the UK; in the USA it is known as Caspia. Asparagus fern is good and is very fine, therefore more useful in the smaller scales.

A belt and braces approach is needed when using these fine natural materials. To keep them from drying out, give them a good soaking of diluted PVA glue and warm water. This mix should resemble thinned milk: about 75 per cent water. Warm water is used because the flower heads are dried and therefore very brittle. The warm water will be sucked up very quickly, making the stems soft, which allows the PVA to penetrate the cells in the stems. When they dry they will remain reasonably supple. You will find this gives more strength and flexibility over a longer period of use.

COLOURING

Colouring of this material is achieved by spray painting with acrylic paints. Though acrylic paints are not generally the best for modelling, in this instance they are the most suitable. You must make sure that there is adequate ventilation. First spray the branches with a priming coat of either dark grey or black. This will give you a really good base on which to build up the colours. Various shades of green are used on top of this priming coat.

After soaking the Statice in a warm water and PVA mix, let it dry. Spray-paint the bunch a dark colour such as dark grey or black, and then a dark green.

APPLYING THE FOLIAGE

Use a large pin or a pin vice with a No. 58 or 60 drill bit. Lay the trunk on a cutting mat. Starting at the top or pointed end, make holes by drilling or pushing the pin into the balsa. Stagger the holes and make sure they go right through the trunk; referring to photos or drawings of the trees will give you an idea of the density of the branches. Then stand the trunk up and clamp it in a vice (see box overleaf).

Starting from the top, push the branches into the pre-drilled holes and out though the other side. Dip each branch end into PVA glue and clip the ends that project out of the other side back to the trunk. Work your way down the tree, using larger or longer pieces of foliage towards the bottom. Some dead branches can be made with odds and ends of the clippings; these will be nearer the bottom of the tree and don't need to be very long to give the right impression.

You may find it difficult to make lots of holes at the top of the trunk where it comes to a point, so glue the foliage branches directly to the trunk by using quick-drying glue such as UHU or Copydex.

Finally, spray the whole tree with a varnish/matte medium and, to add a little extra detail, sprinkle on a very fine layer of cellulose crumb. This should be done whilst the varnish/matte medium is still wet.

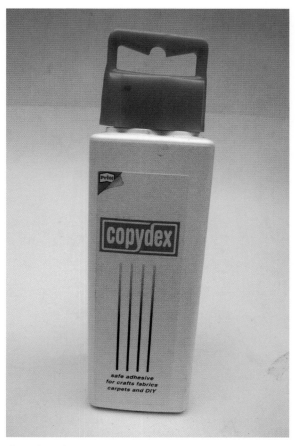

Copydex glue is suitable for this job.

Using Statice to create branches

1. Drill several holes near the top of the trunk.

2. Then cut your Statice to the required length.

3. The top-most pieces of foliage will have to be stuck directly onto the trunk.

4. Dip the end in quick-drying glue and push the end into the hole.

5. The tree is now taking shape.

STATIC GRASS

The use of static grass as an alternative to Statice has proved a revelation. It is excellent for producing trees such as spruce.

Cut some short lengths of fine copper wire and press one end into a piece of polyurethane foam board that is held vertically in a vice. Spray the wires with a green or black paint. Fill the static generator with short fibres, approximately 4mm (⅙in) long. Attach the ground wire of the apparatus to the board and tap the body over the pre-coated wires with the grille about 25mm (1in) away; the paint on the wires has to be wet for the fibres to adhere. They will attach themselves in an orderly manner. Then spray them again with matt varnish or a very strong hair spray. Apply another coat, this time using shorter fibres.

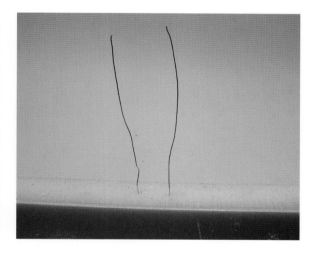

TOP: **Cut some fine wire to length and push one end into a piece of foam board. Spray the wire with a dark green or black paint.**

ABOVE: **The finish is quite remarkable. You could almost stick on some pine cones.**

When you are happy with the result, a final coat of a matte medium or varnish spray can be applied. These are then added to the balsa trunk in the same way as described above.

GENERAL TREE FOLIAGE

There are nearly as many methods of making foliage as there are varieties of tree. Foliage, due to its size, cannot easily be attached directly to the branches so an intermediary is required. This can be postiche (doll's hair), rubberized horse hair, industrial floor scrubbers, polyester fibres, stainless steel wire wool, sea foam or Statice/Caspia (see box overleaf).

In all cases a dark colour is recommended for the carrier. If this is not available, then a quick blow-over with paint will do the trick. It is preferable that the carrier is not seen, or at least that it is as unobtrusive as possible. The actual foliage is made of sawdust, crumbed latex or cellulose, dried tea leaves, static fibres or pre-coloured paper leaves (Selkirk foliage).

POSTICHE

This is an artificial hair produced for the theatre and film industry and brought to the modelling world; it is also called doll's hair or crepe hair. Postiche comes in many colours from blonde through to black, though for modelling use it is best to stick to black, dark brown and grey. It is very curly with a natural tendency to stay that way, and is supplied in plaited lengths. Sometimes postiche is sold in straight shanks, but these are usually brightly coloured and so unsuitable for our purposes.

Pinch a small amount off the end of the plait about 25mm (1in) in length (see box on pp.119–21). Begin by teasing and pulling the hair into a light airy 'ball'. This will stretch out into approximately 50mm (2in) in diameter and in this state becomes almost invisible. This 'ball' is then sprayed with an adhesive: a very sticky and preferably unscented hair spray is good for this, or a well-diluted matte medium. Use a piece of card or similar to catch the back spray and prevent everything in the workshop becoming covered in a sticky film. Use the hair spray as the first 'line of attack' as over the years you will find it

COMMON CARRIER MATERIALS

Postiche, more commonly known as doll's hair.

Polyester. This one has been pre-coloured.

Industrial floor scrubber. These are colour-coded for coarseness: the colour we require is black, as any other colour usually means a less coarse make-up that will not be as useful.

Stainless steel wire wool. This will be sprayed black.

Sea foam. This will be treated with warm water and PVA glue then, when it is dry, sprayed black or dark grey.

USING POSTICHE TO CREATE FOLIAGE

1. Pinch off about 25mm (1in) of the postiche.

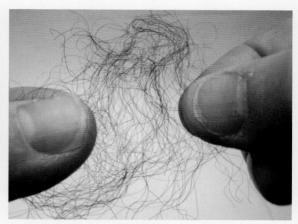

2. Tease this out into a light, airy ball.

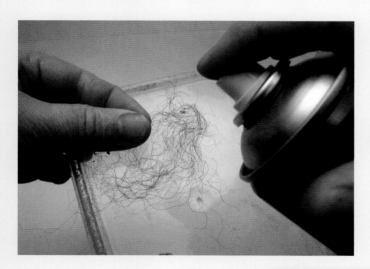

3. Spray the postiche with a tacky hair spray or similar adhesive.

4. Make sure it is well and truly soaked.

continued overleaf

5. Dip the postiche into the crumb and roll it over a few times.

6. Then shake off any loose particles.

7. Fix the foliage to each individual branch and build the tree as Mother Nature would, branch by branch.

8. Work your way up and round the tree, checking the canopy as you go.

9. With the tree nearly complete, a natural and realistic tree has been achieved.

will lose its grip (matte medium or matt varnish would be the second 'line of attack').

The resultant soaked 'ball' is then dropped into a container full of your chosen leaf scatter. Turn this over a few times in the scatter until the postiche is fully covered. This is then given a quick shake and set aside to dry. It is a good idea to 'batch build' these so that when you come to place them on the tree you have a choice from which to pick.

Applying the Postiche-Based Foliage

After smearing or spraying PVA or scenic spray glue over the branches, they are ready to receive the leaves. Carefully spread the foliage over the tree, starting at the bottom and working your way around and up the tree. This method will enable you to create a light and airy tree with a really open canopy; remember to turn it over to check the canopy. Spray the whole tree and, when you are completely happy

RIGHT: It is always a good idea to have photos of real examples close to hand.

Another real example of a tree with a model made for Peter Wiggins' Southern Railway (7mm/O gauge) layout (below).

ABOVE LEFT & RIGHT: **Hold the postiche with a suitable gripping device – in this case a clothes peg. Steam the shank (being careful not to scald yourself) over a kettle. Gently pull the hair down from the top and the postiche will straighten.**

with the shape, apply matt varnish or matte medium and set aside to dry.

Further Methods for Postiche

If your tree is a weeping willow or birch then the postiche is treated in a slightly different way.

Cut a suitable length off the plait. Using a clothes peg or a similar gripping device, steam it over a kettle – be very careful not to scald your fingers. When steaming the postiche always err on the side of caution as to how much postiche you steam in one go. Gently straighten the postiche by pulling the hair from the top. It will be straightened just enough for you to attach your leaves, but not so straight as to be unnatural. Once it has been steamed and semi-straightened, it will not go back to its curly state.

The leaf scatter is applied as described previously. It is attached to the tree in the same way as the other types of foliage but will hang down rather than stay bunched, resembling a weeping tree.

POLYESTER FIBRE

This fine and airy material is used in the furniture and clothing industries. It should be teased out in the man-ner described for postiche. As it is white it will need to be spray painted with either black or a dark grey, set aside to dry and then treated as postiche. It is very good for representing trees with a slightly denser canopy; it stays where you put it and does not droop, and with the use of finer leaf scatter is excellent.

INDUSTRIAL FLOOR SCRUBBERS

This material is probably the best for representing heavy foliated trees. You can purchase it from commercial cleaning suppliers; it comes in either disc shape (as used with floor-scrubbing machines) or as a pad, and is graded from polishing (very fine) right through to scrubbing (very coarse). The latter, which is colour-coded black, is the best for our purposes.

Using the Scrubbers

Begin by cutting a small piece of the pad/disc – about 50×50mm (2×2in) – with a strong pair of scissors. Then pull this apart until the required density is reached.

As this is a very strong material, hair spray is not as good as an adhesive: use a matt varnish or scenic

Cut the scrubber into squares. Pull the square apart until you have the correct density. This is then sprayed with a strong adhesive and covered with your chosen foliage.

spray glue. Sprinkle or roll the whole bunch in a container full of leaf/scatter. Use a strong glue to attach the foliage to the branches: UHU or Copydex (a latex-based glue) or, if a large tree is being modelled, a hot-melt glue gun. As the tree 'grows', so you will see the real shape of the model unfold. Work from the bottom up and remember to check the canopy.

RUBBERIZED HORSEHAIR

This material is also used in the furniture and packing industry. It is treated in the same manner as the industrial floor scrubbers but has to be spray-painted before it is used. It needs a little more work for it to look right, but despite that is a very versatile material.

SEA FOAM

This is a natural material that can be used in the smaller scales to represent whole trees. As sea foam is a natural product it has a tendency to dry out and become brittle. To overcome this you will have to treat it with a weak solution of warm water and PVA or glycerine and water. The method for achieving this is described in the section dealing with natural foliage.

After you have finished treating it and it is dry, break the 'branches' off into small pieces. These will be eventually stuck on to the wire armature of the tree, but first they are sprayed with a dark colour. Give each piece a coat of hair spray or adhesive and sprinkle on or dip into your chosen leaf/scatter.

Once this has been applied, stick each piece on to the branches using reasonably strong glue. Check for shape and spray the whole tree with matt varnish or matte medium. It is beneficial at this time to spray and apply a little scatter to the underside. This works very well if you throw the scatter onto the underside rather than sprinkle: it will unfortunately stick to the trunk of the tree and takes an absolute age to pick it off, but it is still a worthwhile exercise.

LEAVES

SAWDUST

Time has moved on yet sawdust still has its place in modelling. It comes dyed in various shades of green, brown, black and grey. There is very fine sawdust called 'wood flour' that is used mainly for groundwork rather than for leaves. Its main fault is that the larger, coarser grades are not quite as colourfast as one would like. If you are to use this medium, then a fairly strong glue is used and on a fairly rigid carrier. This will give you a dense tree, which will let very little light through. It is most useful as part of a woodland, set mainly in the centre of the wood where it will be disguised by the tree tops around it and so detail is not so important.

LATEX AND CELLULOSE CRUMB

As has been touched upon previously, the colours of this material can be rather bright and will not look natural on the model. You may have to 'let down' their intensity of colour after the tree is complete. Mix up a very weak colour, a shade or two below the one on the tree's foliage, in either acrylic or enamel paint with plenty of water or solvent. Carefully airbrush the foliage, trying not to get too much on the trunk.

If you are making a silver birch tree, which has an open character, a fine crumb should be used. A heavier tree such as a horse chestnut can be replicated with a coarser granulated crumb; this is also used when representing ground cover. The application of the crumb is described in the section on using postiche.

Making Your Own Crumb

If you want to try and make your own crumb the following method can be used (see also box overleaf).

A latex rubber carpet underlay (preferably green) is required. The underlay is cut into small pieces with a pair of scissors and the backing is removed. These pieces are then placed in a small electric coffee grinder and given a few seconds of 'whizz'. Let the granules settle then give them another 'whizz' for a few more seconds, and so on until a fine crumb is reached. This is not as refined, perhaps, as the manufactured crumb and not even the right colour, but it can be spray-painted on the tree once it has been attached to its carrier.

PAPER LEAVES (SELKIRK FOLIAGE)

These leaves are finely chopped, dyed paper. The best way to apply them is to put your carrier on the branches, then spray the carrier with adhesive and sprinkle

Paper leaves (Selkirk foliage). These are very good, but they are not colourfast so they have to be treated carefully when water-based spray adhesives are used.

*ABOVE: **Tea bags and loose tea will need to be thoroughly washed and dried before use.***

*RIGHT: **Latex or cellulose crumbs:** probably the most common medium in use today.*

*BELOW: **Static fibres:** a revelation when pine trees such as spruce are being modelled.*

The less common dyed sawdust.

MAKING LATEX CRUMB FROM CARPET UNDERLAY

The DIY method of producing scatter, using a coffee grinder to turn underlay that has been cut into small pieces and deprived of their backing into crumb.

the paper leaves on to this. Their only drawback is that they are not colourfast with certain adhesives. My advice is to experiment with various glues/adhesives. They therefore have to be treated carefully but, once on the tree and fixed with varnishes or fixatives, they give a really good impression of leaves.

'REAL' LEAVES

You can use loose tea leaves or dried-out leaves from used teabags. They are very good for representing the leaf mulch in woodland scenes.

Wash out the teabags after they have been used to make sure that all the tannin has been diluted. Leave the bags to dry, then open them up and spread the contents out on to an old baking tray to make sure they are thoroughly dry. Leaves from teabags are especially good around the bases of the trees and even as a few stubborn dead leaves on a winter tree that haven't fallen yet. A beech tree looks good with

Dried, used tea leaves as mulch in a woodland scene in 7mm/O gauge.

a few of these left on the branches. Loose-leaf tea is better for the larger scales as it is somewhat larger. Like teabags, this tea must be washed to remove tannin and then dried out.

Once the leaves have been placed in your scene you must 'fix' them with either a good matt varnish or matte medium. Be very careful if the tea leaves have been applied to branches, as the force of the spray may knock them off.

STATIC FIBRES

Static fibres are good at representing pine needles, and are applied with the aid of a puffer bottle or a static generator. There are numerous shades and colours so be careful in picking the right shade. They mostly have a glossy finish, which will tend to make the model look toy-like. This can be overcome by giving the tree a light dusting of a matt varnish.

IVY

Much seen but rarely modelled, ivy plays a very big part in a landscape scene. It can be found on buildings, walls, fencing, on the ground and on trees. Depending on which scale you are modelling, the representation of ivy is done in two distinct ways, one using latex and cellulose crumb the other using a natural product that comes dyed in various shades of green from scenic suppliers.

USING THE LATEX CRUMB

In the smaller scales use postiche as a carrier for the ivy. Pinch the postiche off the end of the plait and, instead of teasing it into a ball, tease it to a longish length. Spray this with hair spray and drag it through the correct colour crumb to a density that represents ivy. Glue it to the trunk of the tree when it has dried: start at the top and carefully weave it down and around the main branches. It will remain on the trunk without any glue if handled carefully. Once you have it in position, spray everything with matt varnish.

The same system applies wherever ivy is required except on buildings, where a slightly different approach is employed. Before the ivy is applied a quick squirt of matt varnish to the brick or stonework is

Much seen but rarely modelled, ivy is everywhere.

Latex crumb and postiche created the ivy growing up this tree.

required. Lay the ivy onto the wet medium and follow up with a final fixing of either matt varnish or matte medium.

NATURAL IVY PRODUCT

These natural leaves are best used for the larger scales – they are a heavier product. Apply them to teased-out floor scrubbers or polyester fibre; the latter should be sprayed black or dark brown. This time using stronger spray glue, the leaves are sprinkled on and left to dry before being glued to the model. Copydex is quite good for sticking the ivy to your model. Care is needed when painting on the glue: make sure you apply the smallest amount, then let it dry to a light, tacky feel. Press the ivy onto this with the lightest of touches. If you are too heavy-handed, the fila-

ments will become flat and the airy nature of the ivy will be lost. The whole thing is sprayed with a matte medium to hold it in place.

PLANTING THE TREE

Earlier in this chapter we discussed the tap root. Whether your tree is going to be removable or permanently planted, that piece of brass you soldered onto the copper wire armature/skeleton now comes into play.

Set a short length of tubing that has an inside diameter the same as the outside diameter of the tap root into the landscape. Make sure it is well seated and solid before planting your tree. Spread any surface roots that you have showing and plug the tree into the socket.

A typical setting – how we would like to remember those summer days when we were young and everything was rosy. This model was originally built by Stephen Brown in 1991 and I had the pleasure of owning it and remodelled it in 2007. The scale is 7mm:ft with a 9mm track gauge. The larger trees have Selkirk foliage for their leaves and the smaller ones have latex crumb.

Warm up the hot-melt glue gun and draw the molten glue over the wire roots, adding a few more as necessary by moving the gun away from the wire and trickling the glue over the ground to form a convincing root system.

Let the glue cool and proceed to paint these roots with a fairly thick decorative plaster mix.

Let all the work dry and then paint them with a water-based paint, matching the colour to the bark on the tree.

This natural product is useful for the larger scales, and the inset shows how it has been put to use on a 7mm scale tree.

CHAPTER SIX

FENCES, WALLS & HEDGES

FENCING

The railway companies of the past developed their own distinctive styles of fences, and by looking at the fencing you could generally tell which company owned that piece of land. The Midland Railway (later part of LMS and then British Rail's LMR) had diagonal fencing, while the Southern Railway had concrete post and concrete panels.

The main styles of fencing are adequately covered by the major model railway manufacturers, and by following their instructions a very adequate fence can be made. To alter or change the look of these fences you can add a few brambles and perhaps some creeping vegetation.

The patchwork quilt of the countryside. The hedgerows have many large trees breaking the line; these would, in years gone by, have been the edge of a much larger wood.

Fencing typifies ownership of railway land, in this case the Midland Railway (recreated with Slater's Plastikard).

WALLS

THE DRY-STONE WALL

This is a vast subject and only the trained eye can recognize which part of the country they are in by looking at the dry-stone walls. The type of stone will dictate the style of walling, though the principles for building a wall of this kind remain the same wherever you are. Some areas, however, have very few drystone walls, if any: the local stone where I live is called Kent Rag and really does not lend itself to the craft.

The wall here is not dry-stone, but a Kent Rag stone bonded with a lime and grit mortar. This kind of wall would surround a church – as in this case – or a farmyard. Many buildings in the area would be made of the same, local stone.

The waller's art taken to the highest degree: what a challenge for the modeller!

When most of these walls were built stone was a cheap and readily available material. Landowners would clear the stones and small boulders from the land so they could plough the ground and allow livestock to graze; the stone that was cleared was then used to build the walls to keep livestock in and intruders out. The dry-stone waller became a skilled and much sought-after craftsman.

There are many miles of walls that have lasted for centuries and have needed very little maintenance. The craftsmen of the past could build walls absolutely anywhere: mountains, fells and moors did not deter them and in the more scarcely populated areas of the UK one can find dry-stone walls in the most inhospitable environments.

The style and type modelled will demarcate the area. In the Peak District in Derbyshire and the Yorkshire Dales, the land is like a patchwork quilt of walls, the styles of which are quite different. Likewise the walls that mark out the land in south-west Scotland differ enormously from those in north-east Scotland. In the north-east they tend to be granite and were built to keep cattle from straying. The stones in these walls are of a regular shape and tremendous weight, making it easier to run straight courses. Because of their regularity there was less need for coping stones: if there were any, they were massive granite blocks weighing anything up to 50kg (over 100lb). Imagine having to lift these on to the top of a newly constructed wall!

Some dry-stone walls were built as a single skin with daylight showing through the courses. This was a deliberate ploy by the waller and farmer alike, as it looked unsafe to the livestock who would otherwise have tried to jump or climb over it. Most of the solid dry-stone walls will have a taper to them, being narrower at the top than the bottom.

Finally, the colour carries a lot of information: for instance the honey-coloured Cotswold stone would not look right in the north-west of Scotland with its dark granite, and vice versa.

DRY-STONE WALLS FROM AIR-DRYING CLAY

This method is very time consuming, but it produces a truly realistic-looking wall and is particularly useful when the wall is close to the viewer. It is much better to model small sections at any one time.

Place a small sheet of polythene on the landscape where the wall is going to be built, to form the foundation of the wall. This will allow the wall to follow the contours of the land.

Begin by pinching a small amount of air-drying clay from the pack. Roll this between the thumb and forefinger to form little balls or pellets about the size of a small pea. As the clay will dry very quickly, work has to be fairly rapid. The first course is then lightly pressed into a neat bed of PVA glue that has been spread on the polythene.

DIFFERENT STYLES OF DRY-STONE WALL

How do they stand there? Note the small packing pieces and the coping stones. The stones here are just laid on top of the wall, and not really picked out to stand on edge.

LEFT & BELOW:
This wall has specifically been built as a retaining wall with a good bond and a strong coping. Some mortar has been used in a patch repair, but this is rare and is difficult to see.

continued overleaf

This wall is made from Mendip stone and makes for a neat appearance when carried out correctly.

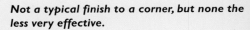

Not a typical finish to a corner, but none the less very effective.

LEFT & OPPOSITE PAGE TOP LEFT & TOP RIGHT:
Two variations in coping stones. The first is typical of Somerset (Mendip) and the second of the Yorkshire Dales. The third one shows a neat and tidy wall end and return.

BELOW: *A drainage hole: so often seen, but not often modelled.*

BELOW RIGHT: *An animal 'through' or 'creep' hole will allow sheep to pass from one field to another without the need to open gates and can be (as in this case) closed off very easily.*

Building a dry-stone wall from air-drying clay

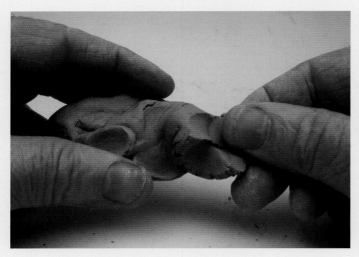

1. Pinch off a small amount of air-drying modelling clay.

2. Roll the clay into small pellets about the size of a small pea.

3. Start by laying some pellets lightly pressed together.

4. When you have reached the required height, gently press and pat the stones to compact them.

5. Pinch off a further piece of clay, then roll and flatten it to form a flat stone.

continued overleaf

6. Place these coping stones on edge or as required. Keep the top of the wall damp during this process.

Each course is built up much as a dry-stone wall would be built in real life. For the larger scale, modellers make two skins with a little batter (slope) to make the wall appear narrower near the top. This doesn't need to be very much, but it will give a real feel to the model. When reaching a steeper drop, try to keep the courses as level as possible, much as the waller would do.

Once the model has reached the right height, the coping stones can be added along the top edge. You will need to keep the wall a little damp for this to be done. Before you add the coping stones, press lightly down on the structure so that all is bonded together.

The coping stones are made by squashing the little pellets until they are almost completely flat; their precise form depends on the stone and the area being modelled. The coping stones are set in place by gently pressing them into the damp wall. With a touch of water on a paint brush, mould the bottom of the coping stone into the top course of the wall. Gently pat the sides with a palette knife: it will squash the pea-like pellets slightly, giving them a more realistic shape.

The finished end to a wall is very important and should show the correct bonding. If there is a field gate, a 'hiker's through' (sometimes called a 'squeeze stile') or a step stile, this will need a little extra care.

The squeeze stile or hiker's through is usually represented by the dry-stone wall being properly returned and a large vertical stone placed in the ground at a slight angle; the same thing applies on the other side, so that the two large vertical stones form a V. This is achieved by rolling a longer piece of air-drying clay, patting it flat and shaping it with a palette knife. Plant this against the end of the wall with a touch of PVA glue.

Where a step style is being modelled, larger stones are made. They must be wider than the wall and are laid horizontally so they project through either side of the wall, much like a staircase. The top two or three courses are left off, and no coping stones are required. Once everything has dried and settled, brush the wall with an old tooth brush. By brushing the wall all superfluous knobs and the like will be taken off. This process will 'age' the wall by putting a fine grain effect on the stones.

You can represent a wall that has not been maintained as it should have been and has begun to collapse by breaking out a small part of the model and placing a small pile of stones on either side of the model. Then perhaps a cheap or temporary repair by the farmer can be replicated by a fence post or two with barbed wire put across the hole.

RIGHT & BELOW:
A step stile can make an interesting break in a wall, particularly if at or near to the front of the model. Carefully mould some clay into fairly large stones and press these on both sides of the wall with a touch of PVA, or build them in as you go.

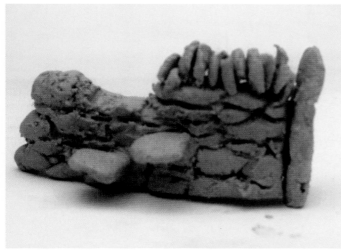

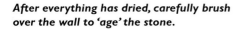

After everything has dried, carefully brush over the wall to 'age' the stone.

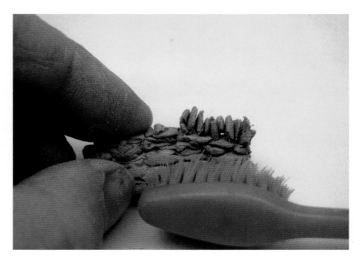

Painting the Wall

To paint the wall use water-colours, starting with a very dark colour. Float the colour into the joints to show up any imperfections in the stones, as well as the courses. Follow this with a general colour for the stone. Then pick out any individual stones just to give that extra bit of detail and interest. Once all this has dried, carefully remove the polythene and glue the wall in place using a hot-melt glue gun or strong quick-drying glue.

SOLID AIR-DRYING MODELLING CLAY WALLS

This approach is used for short sections of wall perhaps around a farmyard or churchyard, or even the backs of terraced housing.

Form a block of modelling clay to the height of the wall, including the coping stones. Smooth this out, making it as straight as you can with the aid of a little water. Lay it on its side on a piece of glass or plastic sheet. Starting at the bottom, scribe joints into the clay with an engineer's scribe or something that has a sharpened tip. Be careful to keep the surface damp, as it will dry fairly rapidly. Make sure there are no straight joints (vertical joints that run from the top to the bottom of the wall). They should be avoided at all times as they show a weakness in the wall. The coping stones are cut across the top of the wall with a modelling knife, preferably one with a worn-out blade as sharpness is not a prerequisite here.

A length of wall can be made in small sections, each section being glued down individually. The end of each section is left blank and with slight indents, something like a rebate; this way, when the sections are stuck together the joint can be disguised. This is achieved by pressing into the rebate a piece of clay that is then scribed to match. When it is all dry, give the completed wall a quick brush-over with an old tooth brush and paint it with water-colours.

'DEPRON' DRY-STONE WALL

Depron is a high-density lightweight polystyrene board used by model aircraft hobbyists. It comes in sheet form and from 2–6mm in thickness; it is extremely good for scribing and will take acrylic paints well.

1. Solid block dry-stone walls.

2. Form a solid block of clay the height of the wall including the coping stones.

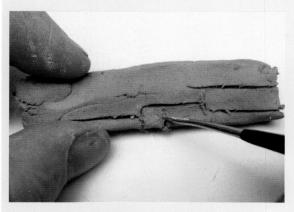

3. Scribe the stones whilst the clay is still slightly damp.

4. *Be careful to avoid straight vertical joints.*

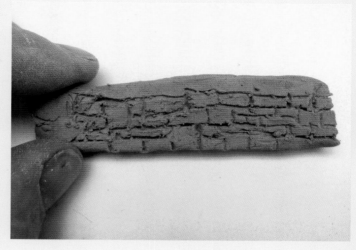

5. *The ends of the wall should be finished with a good bond.*

6. *Cut the coping stones using a craft knife or similar; a sharp blade is not necessary.*

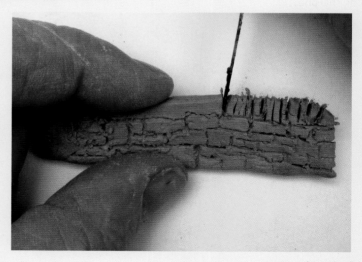

continued overleaf

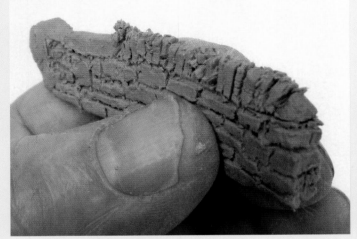

7. *The finished wall before the brushing.*

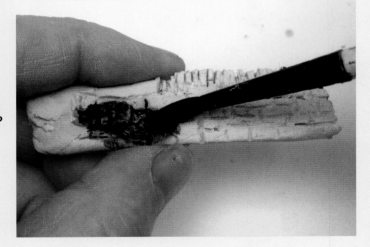

8. *A wash of a dark colour will bring out the detail in the stones. When this is dry, start to pick out individual features.*

9. *The finished solid clay wall.*

Depron walls are quick to make and, if accurately scribed, will look quite convincing. Always make sure you use a sharp blade when cutting Depron, as a blunt blade will drag the edge and the finish will be wholly unacceptable.

Depron is a lot quicker to use than the aforementioned methods, but when finished is none the less quite realistic.

To make the wall fit the landscape (especially if it is hilly), begin by holding a pre-cut piece of Depron vertically. Open a pair of dividers out across the gap at the lowest point of the landscape. Next, place the opened dividers at the 'top of the hill' and, keeping the points pressed against the landscape, draw the dividers down the hill to the bottom of the sheet.

Place the sheet flat on the work bench and cut along the scribed line. Open the dividers to the chosen height of the wall and, resting one point against the cut edge, draw a parallel line across the sheet. Cut along that line with your scalpel or craft knife. Make sure the blade is very sharp as the Depron will drag against a blunt blade and destroy any sharp edge you may wish to have.

With a sharp pencil or engineer's scribe, draw the stones onto the surface, remembering to keep the courses as parallel as possible. If there is a very steep incline, try to keep the courses horizontal. Scribe the other side of the Depron sheet in a similar manner, trying to match the courses as closely as possible; of course, if the back side of the wall is not seen, then any detail is irrelevant.

If a thicker wall is required, then scribe two skins and stick them back-to-back with a small spacer at the bottom to give a batter to the wall. Use Copydex or a solvent-free adhesive to do this.

The coping stones are then scribed in and suitable cuts made to represent the edge-on appearance of the stones. Any additional features such as 'throughs' or 'creep holes' (which allow sheep to pass from field to field) can be scribed and cut out. Any returns on the ends of the walls, stiles and so on can be fabricated and stuck on as a retro fit.

Painting the Walls

Painting Depron requires a slightly different approach as it is not porous. A priming coat is needed, which usually consists of an acrylic paint the shade of which will match the underlying stone colour.

Make sure all the surfaces are covered with the primer, including all the joints. After it has dried apply a coat of a thinned mix of black/dark grey acrylic paint to the courses – the capillary attraction draws the diluted paint along the courses. Once this has dried, paint the individual stones. Details such as ferns growing out of joints are easily added later on. These can be made from latex/cellulose crumb and/or static fibres.

MAKING DEPRON WALLS

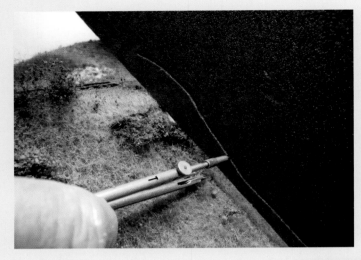

1. To make the wall fit the landscape (especially if it is hilly), begin by holding a pre-cut piece of Depron vertically. Take a pair of dividers and open them out across the gap at the lowest point of the landscape. Next, place the opened dividers at the 'top of the hill' and, keeping the points pressed against the landscape, draw the dividers down the hill to the bottom of the sheet.

2. Place the sheet flat on the work bench and proceed to cut along the scribed line. Open the dividers to the chosen height of the wall and, resting one point against the cut edge, draw a parallel line across the sheet.

3. Cut along that line with your scalpel or craft knife. One point here, make sure the blade is very sharp as the 'Depron' will drag against a blunt blade and destroy any sharp edge you may wish to have.

4. With a sharp pencil or engineer's scribe, draw the stones onto the surface, remembering to keep the courses as parallel as possible.

5. The wall will sit comfortably on the hillside and can be fixed with a solvent-free adhesive.

MORTAR-BUILT PRESSED STONE WALLS

Although not representative of any particular style of stone wall, this method is very useful and a quick way of creating a long length of wall. It is created by making a mould, which is pressed into the wet modelling clay. This can be a standalone wall or glued to a card heart.

Making the mould is simplicity itself, but the work *must* be carried out in a well-ventilated area as it involves melting styrene board. Cut a block of styrene foam to 70mm long by 30mm wide by 25mm thick (2¾ × 1¼ × 1 in).

Fabricate an extension to a soldering iron with a piece of brass that has a small, flat area the size of the iron tip; this extension is used to dissipate some of the heat from the iron, over which it is slipped. Alternatively, use an old tip on an iron with the temperature turned right down. When the iron is hot, dab the tip into the edge of the styrene block: after a little practice you will see how long you need to hold the iron in the styrene. This will make irregular holes that can be left as they are or, by moving the iron, elongated to represent larger stones.

Try to avoid straight joints. Work your way across the block until the whole area is covered, taking some stone indents off the edge of the block: this will give a staggered joint when the next impression is made. The space between these holes will look like pointed mortars, after you have made the impression.

1. Dip the hot soldering iron into the styrene block's edge. With a little practice you will soon see how long to leave the iron on the styrene. Move the iron around to make larger indents to represent bigger stones.

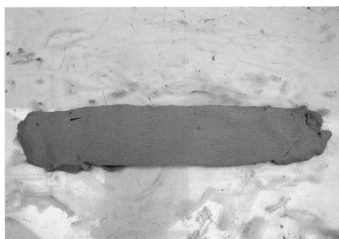

2. Press a piece of modelling clay onto a sheet of glass.

3. Push the mould into the wet clay, working your way along to the end. On each pressing, match the joint as carefully as you can. *Make several of these impressions in one session and leave them to dry. Then remove the strips of walling and glue them to a heart of card, or back-to-back as described for the Depron wall system.*

Lay a piece of plate glass on the bench and press a piece of modelling clay onto the glass. Whilst this clay is still wet, press the mould block into the clay. Work your way along the clay until the end is reached.

Make several more pieces like this, leaving them on the glass plate until they are dry. They can then be lifted off and either stuck back to back, as described in the Depron section, or on to a card heart, making a reasonable representation of a wall.

STANDALONE PRESSED WALLS

The same can be done with thicker pieces of modelling clay. Work up a piece of clay to the required height and thickness, remembering to put a little batter to the sides. Stand it up on the plate-glass bed and impress the wall using two moulds, sandwiching the clay between them and working your way along as described previously. Flatten the top with a knife and then proceed to make and bed the coping stones, as described earlier in this chapter. They are then glued on with PVA and, when all is dry, give the wall a good brushing with a toothbrush.

RETAINING WALLS

Embossed plastic and card sheets have been available from various manufacturers for many years and represent good value for money. They cover a vast array of different styles, from dressed stone to cut, square-edged stone walls with regular joints. However, situations may arise where you have to make your own

because suitable products aren't available for a specific requirement.

A good foundation is important and for this foamboard is recommended; this is a card-faced styrene sandwich. A thin MDF or hardboard such as the type used for backing pictures in picture frames is also very handy. The hardboard should be used with the smooth face to the back of the work. Start by cutting the backing to shape and checking its fit on the model.

Lay the board on a flat surface and prime the back with either PVA or paint. This coating will act as a balance to the air-drying clay on the front and will reduce any tendency to curl or distort.

Paint neat PVA glue onto the surface and, whilst this is still wet, press the air-drying modelling clay into it. After the whole area is covered, smooth it over with a wetted thumb or a palette knife and leave it to dry. When the clay has cured give the face a light sanding with a 150 grit glass paper.

Set the stone courses out with a soft pencil: a harder lead will mark the surface too deeply, and if any mistakes are made these will be harder to erase. When you are happy with the general layout, scribe the pencilled-in stonework with an engineer's scribe or suitably sharpened tool. This is a time-consuming method, but in the end very satisfying.

External corners are finished with either a straightforward bonding on the return or by quoining: this is large dressed stones or similar set with an alternate head and stretcher pattern. The work is then coloured using water-based paint.

Embossed or moulded plastic sheet can be useful in certain situations. This particular piece is made with Slater's Plastikard and has had a thin coat of a pre-coloured plaster mix.

MAKING A RETAINING WALL FROM AIR-DRYING CLAY

1. Coat both sides of the backing with PVA glue to balance out the tension formed by the coatings. If you don't do this, the backing will bend and ruin all your hard work.

2. After you have spread the air-drying clay over the backing and smoothed it over with a palette knife, let it dry. Lightly sand the surface and set out the stonework with a soft pencil.

3. Begin to scribe the stonework.

4. Scribe in any quoining or straightforward stone returns.

continued overleaf

5. Make sure the bonding works out correctly for the end returns.

6. Brush over the whole wall with a toothbrush and paint.

LEFT & BELOW: **7.** The finished retaining wall.

HEDGEROWS

Hedgerows are, like dry-stone walls, a good barrier for keeping in stock and demarking boundaries, and generally taken for granted. They need little maintenance save an annual trim, usually carried out in late winter or the early spring.

To represent hedgerows in the autumn and winter months requires quite a bit of work as usually all that can be seen is bare 'twiggery'. An exception to the rule is the evergreen holly, which, as a hedgerow tree, is probably more common than is generally realized. It will stand and grow above the normal hedge height if not cut down regularly.

If you put the hedgerow in the foreground of your model, a great deal more detail will be required, and about as much work is needed to create a realistic-looking hedgerow as to create a 'naked' winter tree. Spring and summer hedgerows are much easier to make. There is a wealth of detail that can be added to a summer hedgerow, with many shades of green along with flowers on top as well as at the base.

You can occasionally use a hedge as an excuse to cover an unfinished model as maybe Mother Nature would do, creeping in to cover over a wall or derelict building.

INDUSTRIAL FLOOR SCRUBBERS

There are several ways to make hedgerows in the smaller scales. One such way is the use of industrial floor scrubbers, as described in Chapter 5.

Cut a floor scrubber to a rough size using a heavy pair of scissors, pulling and teasing out the dense matting as you go, trimming and shaping the hedge with the scissors. Spray small areas near the top a dark shade of brown and, as the floor scrubber is black, leave the base in that colour – the brown colour is used to represent new growth. Apply a spray adhesive to the whole hedge and sprinkle it with a scatter material. Then fix the hedge down onto the model using either a hot-melt glue gun, UHU or a thick bed of PVA. Sprinkle more crumb at the base.

For any flowers that are needed, lightly spray with adhesive/hair spray, apply a very small sprinkling of colour, and then spray again with varnish or hair spray.

For the larger scales, more work is needed on the scrubbers. Vary the colour and texture of the leaves: paper leaves (Selkirk) is extremely good for this.

Adding Extra Detail

Pinch off some postiche (doll's hair) and tease it out. Spray it with hair spray and drop it into a container of latex or cellulose crumb. Roll it over a couple of times, give it a quick shake, tease it out again and lay this across the top of the hedge. Smaller detail such as flowers can then added whilst the adhesive is still wet. Don't put too much colour on: all you need is an impression of the relevant flower colour. What that colour is will depend, as mentioned earlier, on the time of year and the type of plants you may want to represent.

Another method is to take a small piece of floor scrubber and tease it out until it is almost single-stranded. Then treat it by laying it over the hedge as above with the postiche, or drape it over a wall, fence or the ground. A further application of adhesive/varnish will fix it. This is the best method for brambles e.g. blackberries and wild roses.

A word of caution about acrylic varnishes: some have a whitish finish when they dry, so you must be careful where the varnish is used, experimentation is highly recommended.

Gorse is a little easier in this sense: the pinched-out scrubber is sprayed with adhesive, dipped into the green crumb and sprayed again. Whilst this is still wet, a small pinch of yellow is sprinkled over the 'plant'. The plant is fixed down using a hot-melt glue gun or strong glue.

Foliage can be draped over a fence to further enhance the scene.

The plant can be made in the same way as the 'twiggery' described in Chapter 5 with the exception that the branches start very close to the base of the trunk. These branches can then be bent to form a wall-like shape. The plant is then coated and the foliage applied: it is better to add this bit by bit, as too heavy a canopy will not be right for a winter hedge.

COPPER WIRE AUTUMN/WINTER HEDGE

Pre-form the hedge from copper wire in a similar manner to making a naked tree. Twist fine wires together to make a tree in miniature, as described under 'Fine Multi Strand Wire' in Chapter 5.

Make the branches more horizontal with an obviously short trunk. Each plant will have a lot more spreading branches and they will be much closer together. The branches will need to start very low down the trunk. These branches can be twisted off all round the trunk, and then bent back to form a wall-like appearance.

Touch-solder all the intersections and paint everything with either a decorative plaster mix (this mix should have a little PVA added) or 'Flexi-Bark'. Whether

it should be painted or not will depend on the colour of the bark when it has dried. If the overall colour is mid-grey, leave it as it is: this will look suitably winter-like. Remember to leave enough wire to form a 'tap root'.

If the hedge is to represent a beech or hornbeam, then a few leaves may still be left on the branches: dried tea leaves or Selkirk foliage will come in useful here. Spray the hedge with a strong adhesive and sprinkle a small amount of the tea leaves onto the branches. Build the amounts up slowly, checking the density as you go. To have a too-heavily foliated plant will not look right, as there will be some leaf drop during the autumn and through the winter. It would be better to batch-make these plants for consistency and plant them when everything has dried.

CHAPTER SEVEN

CONCLUSION

During the writing and compiling of this book I have come to realize just how much there is out in the natural world to be modelled. It cannot all be put onto a model, but there is no harm in suggesting some of the detail of Mother Nature in all her glory.

The descriptions and photos in this book should be sufficient for your guidance. If you feel that it is not perhaps quite the way you would do things, that's still good, for it has surely made you look at your work from a different view point.

'Wigleton', an EM gauge layout that was perhaps my first real attempt at an exhibition model railway. It was made in the early 1980s and shown at exhibitions throughout that decade and into the early 1990s.

My inspiration has come from people like the late Jack Kine who, in his kindly manner, encouraged me on to greater things. Reading about and looking at the work of George Iliffe Stokes with his ideas on tree making (I am sad not to have met him) influenced me a great deal. Many customers over recent years have made me stretch myself, creatively speaking, and my own inquisitive mind has made me search out and study more and more the landscape around me.

I hope this book has given you that same inspiration to go out and take a fresh look at your world, and in some small way fired the imagination. After all the work you have put into your locos and rolling stock, don't they deserve to be shown off in a realistic natural scene? To lose ourselves in our model railways, surely, is our

The author in relaxed mood at an exhibition.

Here is my O Gauge (7mm:ft) railway 'Durselyish (A Winters Tale)' on show with all the glory of naked trees, a scene set in early winter.

All of the methods described in this book, with the exception of water, have been used to create this model.

'A cold chill descends over the wood.'

The ivy and crows nests go to make a life-like feel to the tree.

This oak tree has the added detail of a squirrel running up the trunk; if you look closely it is just below the lower branch in the centre of the trunk.

aim? The old motto 'If at first you don't succeed, try, try and try again' is never more apt than in our hobby and especially in landscape modelling. I would urge you not to give up if things don't quite go to plan and to always keep an eye on the natural world, it is full of surprises.

Take a look 'outside the box' and plunge into the world of landscape modelling: you may surprise yourself.

Enjoy your modelling.

LEFT: *Summer's day on 'The Snowdrop Railway', an OO Gauge (4mm:ft) model.*

BELOW: *'Peace, perfect peace': this is perhaps what we all aim for on our model railways. This model was built to span two layouts, giving a scenic break between them.*

SUPPLIERS OF MATERIALS

Greenscene
60 Hollymount
Worcester WR4 9SF

Tel: +44 (0)190 524298
Website: www.greene-scene.co.uk

Realistic Modelling Services
49 Guildford Avenue
Whitfield
Dover CT16 3NG

Tel: +44 (0)1304 825849
Email: kjwarren49@ntlworld.com
Website: www.realisticmodelling.com

Deluxe Materials
Unit 13
Cufaude Business Park
Cufaude Lane
Bramley
Hampshire RG26 5DL

Freephone orders (UK only) tel: 0800 298 5121
Tel: +44 (0)1256 883944
Fax: +44 (0)1256 883966
Email: info@deluxematerials.com
Website: www.deluxematerials.com

Squires Tools
This company carries all of the Greenscene range and many of the tools used for model making. A very comprehensive catalogue is available.

Website: www.squirestools.com

Homecrafts
PO Box 38
Leicester LE1 9B

Tel: +44 (0)116 2697733
Fax: +44 (0)116 2697744
Website: www.homecrafts.co.uk

Rapid Electronics Limited
Severalls Lane
Colchester
Essex CO4 5JS

Website: www.rapidonline.com

General Points
'Artex' or decorative plaster is available from all good building, decorating and DIY supply companies.

Plastic sheet (for modelling water) is available from all good building and DIY supply companies.

All good art supplies and modelling shops will carry a few materials, so check them out also. A trawl of the internet will also yield results.

INDEX